Teaching Students to Write

The Dynamics of Writing Instruction series

Argument

Essays That Define

Comparison/Contrast Essays

▶ **Personal Narratives**

Research Reports

Fictional Narratives

Peter Smagorinsky
Larry R. Johannessen
Elizabeth A. Kahn
Thomas M. McCann
with Joanna L. Anglin

HEINEMANN
Portsmouth, NH

Heinemann
361 Hanover Street
Portsmouth, NH 03801–3912
www.heinemann.com

Offices and agents throughout the world

Library of Congress Cataloging-in-Publication Data
Teaching students to write personal narratives / Peter Smagorinsky . . . [et al.].
    p. cm.
  Includes bibliographical references.
  ISBN-13: 978-0-325-03397-6
  ISBN-10: 0-325-03397-8
  1. English language—Composition and exercises—Study and
teaching (Secondary). 2. Education—Biographical methods.
I. Smagorinsky, Peter.

LB1631.T3327 2012
808'.0420712—dc23   2011041653

Editors: Anita Gildea *and* Lisa Luedeke
Development editor: Alan Huisman
Production: Sonja S. Chapman
Cover design: Monica Ann Crigler
Typesetter: Valerie Levy / Drawing Board Studios
Manufacturing: Steve Bernier

Printed in the United States of America on acid-free paper

16 15 14 13 12 PAH 1 2 3 4 5

CONTENTS

Preface

Despite all the attention that writing instruction received during the final decades of the twentieth century, the teaching of writing in middle and high schools remains, at best, uneven. National Writing Project sites have conducted countless summer institutes, and new books about the teaching of writing appear routinely in publishers' catalogues. Yet assessments continue to find that students' writing is less accomplished than teachers might hope. Undoubtedly, the assessments themselves are not what they ought to be (Hillocks 2002). But even those with relatively good reputations, such as the National Assessment of Educational Progress, find that students in the United States are not writing as well as many people expect them to. What's going on here? And will yet another book about teaching writing make a difference?

We have written this series of small books in the hope that they will provide alternatives for teachers who are dissatisfied with teaching five-paragraph themes, traditional grammar lessons, and other form-driven writing approaches. This book employs what we call a *structured process* method, an approach developed by George Hillocks during his years as a middle school English teacher in Euclid, Ohio, during the 1960s. Hillocks and his students have researched this method and found it highly effective (Hillocks, Kahn, and Johannessen 1983; Lee 1993; Smagorinsky 1991; Smith 1989). In a comprehensive research review, Hillocks (1986) found that over a twenty-year period, structured process writing instruction provided greater gains for student writers than did any other method of teaching writing.

We have also spent a collective 120-plus years using a structured process approach in our high school English classes. We do not claim that we have discovered the one best way to teach writing;

rather, our goal is to explain in detail a method that we all found successful in our teaching.

What's in This Book?

A brief introduction explains what we mean by personal narrative and also why we believe it's important to teach students to do this kind of writing (as well as the thinking related to it). Chapters 1 and 2 show you *how* to teach students to write personal narrative using structured process instruction; in them we describe classroom teaching strategies, provide a sequence of activities and handouts, and show examples of student work. Chapter 3 provides grade-by-grade suggestions for how to include personal narrative writing in thematic units. Chapter 4 explains the structured process approach to teaching writing and its two main tenets, *environmental teaching* and *inquiry instruction*. This will help you understand why we designed the instruction modeled in this book the way we did; it will also help you design your own units of instruction in the future.

What's in This Series?

There are six books, each following a similar format, each focusing on a different type of writing: personal narrative (the focus of this volume), fictional narrative, essays that define comparison/contrast essays, argument, and research reports. If you find this book useful, you may want to read the others as well.

Why Teach Students to Write Personal Narratives?

Storytelling is common to virtually every culture. In the United States, children from many social classes are exposed to storybooks, family stories, and other narratives from an early age. Even families in which reading plays a limited role tell and act out stories routinely as a way of sharing experience and linking the present to the past. As Jerome Bruner (1986) tells it, narrative expression and "paradigmatic" (or analytic) expression are two of the primary means by which people construct their understandings of the world and relate them to others.

In school, stories are a central means of instruction. In elementary classrooms students gather around a teacher, who somehow is able to maintain eye contact with the kids, hold a picture book up so that everyone can follow it, and read the book to them all at once. The emphasis on storytelling is so great that some educators believe informational reading gets second-class status in school (Duke 2000).

This emphasis on reading stories continues throughout children's formal education, with required English courses focusing on literature. Even today's "multimodal" texts, which incorporate elements such as film, computer graphics, kinesthetic movement, and other vehicles, are narrative representations of experience. Stories are a foundational means of sharing what it means to be human.

Even in disciplines that rely less directly on the imagination, storytelling is central to the curriculum. Although it is often reduced to its nonmoving parts (e.g., facts), history is a narrative of the unfolding of human events; more recently, historians also recognize the ways narrative perspective and bias figure into how history is told and learned (Loewen and Sebesta 2010). Similarly, science is often reduced to Mr. Gradgrind's "facts, facts, facts!" but can also be viewed as a narrative of how nature works and experiments are conducted.

Yet *telling* stories receives far less attention—and the higher the grade level, the less attention. Stories are for kids, it seems, and not for more grown-up adolescents. Bruner (1986) is among the many educators who believe that analytic, factual, and relatively static emphases dominate students' opportunities for expression in school, especially in the upper grades. Students are required to read stories, but then must analyze them rather than tell their own stories. Meanwhile, they co-construct narratives while playing video games, write fanfiction with online collaborators, swap stories with their friends as a way to give their experiences meaning, and write about their experiences on social networking websites and other online media. Something is very wrong with this picture.

Being able to write personal narratives helps students solve both academic and personal problems. This book shows you how to create more space in your classroom for students to tell their own stories. Chapter 1 allows personal narrative to stand by itself in the writing curriculum. Chapter 2 integrates personal narrative instruction with other strands of the curriculum in a thematic unit on a sense of place (see www.coe.uga.edu/~smago/VirtualLibrary/Unit_Outlines .htm#SenseOfPlace for a variety of such units). Chapter 3 provides ways to include personal narrative writing across the secondary school English curriculum.

Preparing students to write well-developed, thoughtful personal narratives is a time-consuming process, for both you and them. A structured process approach is a particularly effective way to teach them to do so. The detailed, systematic lesson sequences in this book help students learn the necessary thinking and writing procedures. They will, we hope, also give you ideas for designing instruction using a structured process approach in other areas of your teaching.

Teaching Personal Narratives
as Stand-Alone Writing

A few years ago, Larry Johannessen was helping a high school English department revise its writing curriculum. Examining the teachers' current courses and talking with them about their writing assignments, he was surprised to discover that most teachers did very little with narrative and descriptive writing. When he asked why, the teachers said students had already done plenty of that in elementary and middle school. Besides, the students needed to prepare for the state writing test, which focused on argumentation, and had to know how to write according to standards expected in college and the real world.

It took quite a bit of discussion to convince these teachers that a good writing curriculum should provide a variety of writing experiences and that writing narratives and descriptions helps students learn important thinking and writing strategies. Writing about personal experiences is an opportunity for students to think about their own lives.

Task Analysis

The goal of this series of lessons is for students to learn how to write a narrative about a significant personal experience that elicits an emotive response from the reader. The narrative should include descriptive details, along with figurative language and dialogue where appropriate, so that the reader feels what the writer felt and senses the impact of the experience vicariously.

It's tempting to assume that because young people have been exposed to stories their whole lives, they know how to write a detailed, vivid, engaging narrative about a personal experience. Knowing the conventions of constructing a story, however, is not enough. Students need to learn *procedures* for generating ideas that fit the story form and its conventions. You can't just ask students to recall a significant experience and write a compelling story. You need to lead them through a sequence of activities that show them how to relate a personal experience narrative in evocative ways.

Before students can write an effective personal experience narrative, they need to learn how to describe events using specific sensory details; choose appropriate, concrete sensory details; and use figurative language. Young writers will also need help generating ideas to write about. Your lessons, then, need to introduce procedures for writing with sensory detail and using figurative language. The lessons must also include social interaction so that students receive immediate feedback on their ideas and approaches. Finally, the procedures need to be learned in accessible activities and then applied to increasingly more complex tasks.

Stage 1. Assessing What Students Know About Narrative

Effective instruction is never based solely on assumptions about students' abilities. A preliminary assessment reveals what your students already know and do not know about personal experience writing.

EPISODE 1.1. Use the following prompt to get a sense of what students know about writing personal narratives:

> Write about a personal experience and its consequences that had an impact on you or someone you know. Be as specific as you can

in describing the event and its consequences or impact. Try to write so that a reader will see what you saw and feel what you felt.

Give students forty-five minutes to write their narratives.

EPISODE 1.2. Analyze your students' narratives and use the resulting information to direct your instruction and guide your instructional decisions. Figures 1–1 and 1–2 are typical student responses. Both compositions were written by students in the same urban high school, the first by an "at-risk" freshman and the second by a "regular" sophomore. While the second composition is longer and contains some specific sensory detail, neither composition is particularly effective at conveying the personal experience in ways that engage readers. These students need to learn *strategies for including key sensory and other details* that will help them convey their experience to readers in more powerful ways.

Figure 1–1. Personal Experience Essay: "Scary Encounter"

One day my girlfriend Swaney and me were walking on a highway, when this car came by and tried to hit us, but Swaney saw the car coming and she screamed and pulled me out of the way. Then, the car turned around and started chasing us and both of us started running and we jumped over the guide rail and rolled down the hill. We ran through a tunnel and at the other end the man was standing there waiting for us so we turned around and ran the other way. We saw a man driving a car that we knew and he took us to the police station and they were after the man and captured him. Later we found out that he was an escaped convict from a prison.

After that I was so scared I couldn't sleep for a few nights and I had bad nightmares. Now I'm real scared of the same spot where that happened and I'll never go back there again.

Figure 1–2. Personal Experience Essay: "Car Wash"

It was a warm and sunny day in the spring. Today was a day I've been looking forward to for a month. Our Lady of Good Counsel was having their car wash and I was going to work at it. I hurried and get ready and called my girl-friend Colleen. As I walked out her door I heard the birds singing and dogs barking. I could smell the sweet odor of a new spring day. I saw young kids outside playing ball and jumping rope already. As we neared the school, we could begin to hear explosions of laughter and shouting. We finally got there and cars were already there. I was the cashier and kept all the money in a dented tin box. I got rather bored watching the money so I asked if I could do something else. Then I got sent to the corner store about five times. Soon I just picked up an old torn rag and started washing and drying any car I saw. When we closed, people started squirting each other with the stringy hoses. After a while, everyone was in the act and we had buckets and cups flying. People got thrown in barrels, and someone filled them with soap. Everyone was completely saturated from head to toe. We finally slowed down and sat on the church steps. We counted the money and tried to get a little drier than we were. We all decided to hold a dance with the money we made and finally split up and returned home. We all had a blast that day and even planned an-other car wash for the future.

Stage 2. Gateway Activity: Promoting Attention to Detail

Often students think they have explained something clearly only to find that other people have trouble following their descriptions or instructions. This activity, in which students describe their left shoe clearly enough so that another student can identify it in a pile of all the students' left shoes, prompts them to pay attention to specific details of mundane objects and describe them clearly, vividly, and distinctively. They are motivated to improve their use of details in the descriptive writing they do in later activities.

EPISODE 2.1. Tell students to place both feet under their desk, out of sight. Ask them to take out a sheet of paper and a pen or pencil. Assign each student a number, from one through the number of students in the class, and tell them to write that number on their paper. (This step allows you to match papers and authors without revealing students' identities.) Then have them, without looking at their left shoe, write a description of it, including as many details as they can remember and being as specific as they can. Their goal is to enable someone else in the class to distinguish their shoe from similar shoes based on their description.

Circulate through the classroom for ten or fifteen minutes while students write their descriptions, continually stressing that they may not sneak a peek at their left shoe. Collect the compositions as students finish them or when time is up.

EPISODE 2.2. Have students put their desks in a circle (or double circle, depending on class size), leaving a space in the middle for a pile of shoes. Give each student a small sticker. Tell the students to take off their left shoe, place it on their desk, and affix the sticker to the toe of the sole. Ask two students to collect all the left shoes, number each sticker (using a range of numbers that don't duplicate the numbers the students wrote on their papers), and put them in a pile in the center of the room.

EPISODE 2.3. Mix all the shoes in the center of the room into a giant "left shoe salad." Redistribute the descriptions the students wrote so that each student gets someone else's. Ask students to read the composition they have been given and then see whether they can find the shoe that matches the description. If someone blurts out, "But, so many of them are just alike; how are we going to pick out the right one?" you can teasingly remind them to pick the *left* one, not the right one! Point out that if the owner has written a good, specific description of the shoe, they should have little difficulty picking out the shoe matching the description.

Have students read the descriptions silently, looking carefully at the details the writer provided. Then ask them, in groups of four or five, to look through the shoes for the one that matches the description. When they think they have found the correct shoe, tell them to return to their desk and write the number of the shoe on the description they were given. Keep this part of the activity moving; it should last no more than three minutes.

EPISODE 2.4. Once all the students have had a chance to find a matching shoe, ask volunteers to read their description while you hold up the shoe they've identified as matching the description. Point out key details that help identify the shoe: color, number of shoelace holes or hooks, prominent scuff marks, discoloration, stains, patterns of wear on the soles, and other identifying characteristics.

Some descriptions will offer few if any specific details that help identify the shoe. For example, the student who reads, "It is a white athletic shoe, and it is fairly new. It is a size 9, I think. There is like a black band around the side of the shoe. I think the shoe probably has some scuff marks on it," will probably not be able to pick out the corresponding shoe, since a number of shoes will fit this vague and general description.

EPISODE 2.5. After matching each shoe to its description, spend a few minutes discussing why some students found the matching shoe and others did not. Most often, students who are able to find the correct shoe have been given a specific description; those who cannot have been working from a description that is brief and vague.

If students complain that the activity isn't fair because they were not allowed to look at their left shoe, remind them that when they write about a personal experience, they have to be able remember specific details related to it, just as you asked them to remember specific details about the shoe they put on their foot that morning and have worn all day. Memory plays an important role in generating specific details that will make a past experience come alive for readers.

Depending on how well the students did on this activity, you may want to give them a second opportunity, this time using their right shoe. Reemphasize the sorts of details that contributed to students' ability to identify the shoes.

Stage 3. Reinforcing the Procedures with a More Complex Task

This activity is a modification of one originally developed by George Hillocks in the early 1970s. We have used it (or variations) with elementary, middle, and secondary students, as well as with novice writers in college and university composition courses. It's a very effective way to help students improve their skills in observation and use specific sensory details and figurative language in their descriptions.

Having begun their descriptive work with something they presumably know quite well—their shoes—students now move on to less familiar objects. We use seashells in the illustration here, but you can use a variety of other objects that look more or less the same, such as potatoes, lemons, small decorative stones, carrots, pine cones, figs, apples, black-and-white close-up photographs of insects, photographs of tropical fish, decorative buttons, and geodes. The general structure of the activity remains the same as that of the gateway activity; the task becomes more complex because the objects are less familiar.

EPISODE 3.1. Beforehand, put together a set of fifteen or so small conch shells, each one between three and five inches long and characterized by brightly colored spirals and a smooth inner surface. (As mentioned above, you can substitute any set of similar-looking objects.) Place a small piece of tape on each shell and number them consecutively. Although all the shells are the same type and have similar colors and spirals, each one is unique in some way: it might be the particular colors or shades of color, the size or exact shape, a chip on one edge, the particular texture, or even the way the spiral is shaped (or misshapen). When students first see the set of shells, they often comment that they all look the same. On closer examination, however, each is unique, and it is their task to explain how.

EPISODE 3.2. Begin by showing a single shell of a type different from the conch shell, such as a scallop shell. Hold it up for everyone to see. Point out that if asked to describe it, many people would probably say something like, "It is kind of flat and kind of a half circle shape. It has ridges and it is sort of pink." Take out a second scallop shell and hold it up next to the original one. "But, as you can see, that description also matches the shell I just put next to it. In fact, you probably can't tell which one I was holding first. If you want to describe that shell so that someone would be able to pick it out from another similar shell, you've got to be more specific than I just was, just as you had to be specific to help someone find your shoe in the previous activity." Offer some details that a writer might use to distinguish one shell from the other: a difference in exact color or shape or in the particular textures in each shell that make up the unique radiating fluted pattern. This sort of *thinking aloud* while solving a writing problem may benefit students who are having difficulty writing clear and distinctive descriptions.

EPISODE 3.3.   Give each group of three or four students one conch shell. Ask them to write a group description of their shell that includes specific details that will allow another group to pick it out from all the other shells. Their description should not simply be a list of traits, although they may wish to create an outline or cluster chart before writing. The goal of the activity is to teach them how to write the description in clear paragraph form.

The opportunity to work with peers is essential. It encourages students to talk through their process of describing things in detail, thus articulating their own ideas and learning from their classmates' contributions. They receive immediate feedback about how to do their work better. By pooling their knowledge, they are better able to apply what they learn to independent tasks later.

Remind students that they are to discuss their shell, make some notes, and then write a coherent description. Give each group a number and tell them to write it at the top of their final description. Tell them that they may not identify the number taped to their shell or describe the piece of tape; they may not write or make marks on their shell; and they may not drop or throw their shell or otherwise create distinctive chips or cracks that are not already there. Their task is to describe the shell as it was when they received it.

Give the groups twenty or thirty minutes to write their descriptions. While they are working, make a two-column list for yourself, aligning the number on each of the shells with the number of the group describing it so you'll know which group has which shell. As students finish, collect the shells and the descriptions.

EPISODE 3.4. Mix up the shells on a table in front of the classroom. To make the problem more interesting, include any leftover shells. Then give each group a description written by another group. Have the groups read the description they have been given and, two groups at a time, come to the table, pick the shell that they think is being described, write the number of that shell on the description, and return to their seats.

While the groups are examining shells in the front of the room, ask groups that have already identified their shell, "Do you think you found the right one? What details were most important in helping you pick it out?" Or, if the group isn't sure they've picked the right shell, ask, "What made it so difficult to find the right shell? What could the writers have done to help you?" Questions like these keep students focused and prompt them to be more reflective about what is necessary to write an effective description of the shell.

EPISODE 3.5. Once all the groups have had an opportunity to pick out the correct shell, ask each group, in turn, to read the description they were given and identify the number of the shell they matched it with. Then have the group that wrote the description say whether or not this is the correct shell.

EPISODE 3.6. When all descriptions have been read, assess the results. Usually, about half of the groups will have picked the correct shell. Ask those groups to explain what qualities in the description helped them do so. They will identify specific details that enabled them to distinguish the correct shell from all the others. Point out and emphasize particularly effective details, as you did with the shoes. If students have used figurative language (and they often do), reinforce this element as well. If the figurative language is more confusing than helpful, ask the students why the analogies do not work. Hold up the shells so that the entire class can see how the writers used specific sensory details, including figurative language, to differentiate their shell from the others.

Before the groups return the descriptions to the writers, ask them to underline the best specific detail, circle one part that was vague or confusing, and write one thing that could be done to improve the description. This step encourages students to reflect on what they have learned and practiced.

This sequence of activities helps students understand why it is important to use specific sensory details and figurative language. It also helps them develop some strategies for using clear and vivid description. Students must observe their shell or other object closely, note specific details, and include them in their description. Those who do not do a very good job see why they need to observe closely and why they need to include specific details in their writing.

You can conduct this activity, using different objects, more than once. The objects you use should compel students to observe carefully and translate their observations into specific details in writing. Each repetition should also provide a greater challenge, requiring more specificity. As the sequence progresses, you might also have students work in pairs instead of groups of four or five, thus reducing the level of support.

Students often take on the corrective role during the lessons. One ninth grader complained that the students who received his group's description should have been able to pick out their shell because the shell had brown spots and the description had specified this detail. A girl in the berated group picked up both the correct shell and the shell the group had thought was correct. She walked over to the boy, held up both shells, and said with exasperation, "Yes, it [holding out the correct shell] has brown spots, but, look, so does this one." Then, she glanced at the table full of shells and said, "They all have brown spots. You've got to be more specific than that." The point was very powerfully made not only to the boy who complained but to the rest of the class. This sort of feedback from peers about the need for clarifying details is often more convincing than corrective instruction from you.

Stage 4. Helping Students Use a Variety of Sensory Details

Most students need help understanding that good descriptive and narrative writing contains many appropriate sensory details. It may also contain similes, metaphors, and effective dialogue to help make an experience come alive. The book in this series on writing fictional narratives describes activities in which students practice using sight and sound details to describe a setting, an action, or a conflict. Some of those activities may be used here to help students learn how to describe a personal experience.

You should also include activities to help students learn how to use sensory details other than sight and sound. Our olfactory sense is capable of discriminating over ten thousand scents. However, despite the large number of scents humans can discriminate, the English language is nearly void of words to describe smells. We do have such words as *fruity, resinous, flowery, spicy, putrid,* and *burnt* to describe major categories of smells. Unfortunately, these words, and a few others, such as *rancid, fecund, acrid, fetid, fragrant, sweet,* and *redolent,* nearly complete our vocabulary of smells in English. And few of these words populate the vocabulary of the typical teenager.

Edgar Allen Poe was a master at using sensory details for effect. Yet in "The Pit and the Pendulum" he barely uses the sense of smell, even though his narrator can see virtually nothing. Poe describes two important odors in terms of the substances that give rise to them: "The vapor of heated iron! A suffocating odor" emanating from the heated walls of the dungeon, and "the peculiar smell of decayed fungus" rising from the pit. His description of smells is limited to including a few general adjectives and naming particular odoriferous objects.

If Edgar Allen Poe had trouble describing smells, your students probably will too. The following activity helps students think of ways to describe smells that go beyond the ordinary. It employs Scratch'n'Sniff stickers, which are available at many supermarkets, office supply stories, drug stores, and teacher stores. They usually come in packs of five to fifteen sheets and are relatively inexpensive. Each sheet has one particular smell such as grape, motor oil, strawberry, peanut butter, pizza, mint, or old shoes, among many others both pleasant and not. When someone scratches the surface of a sticker, the scent comes through very strongly, prompting students to develop strategies for describing it.

EPISODE 4.1. Group students in pairs or trios. Keep the groups small so that everyone will be able to talk through the process of describing odors. Give each pair or trio a "What Is That Smell I Feel?"

activity sheet (see Figure 1–3) and a sticker with a different smell. Go over the directions on the handout, emphasizing that the first question asks them to identify the smell. Also tell students to scratch their sticker vigorously, because that brings out more of the scent.

Figure 1–3. What Is That Smell I Feel?

Name(s) _____, _____, _____

1. Identify the substance that you smell:

2. How does the smell feel? Is it smooth, abrasive, rough? Give at least three words:

3. How does the smell move? Does it creep, surround, push, etc.?

4. Compare the smell to something else that will help describe it:

   The smell is like

5. Combine the best details you have written into a sentence that *identifies* the substance and *describes* its smell. Imagine that you have just entered a place and noticed this smell.

Example: As I opened the door, the rasping stink of the ammonia kicked me in the face.

The first question on the activity sheet focuses students' attention on the smell. Questions 2 and 3 ask students to describe each smell in terms of other sensory perceptions; this process helps extend the students' imagination. Question 4 asks students to compare the smell to something else—to use similes and metaphors to describe the smell. Question 5 prompts students to put their observations into a sentence, since most students have had very little experience in writing descriptions of smells.

If your students are younger or less experienced, *model the process*. Show them how to scratch the sticker to release the strongest aroma, and then lead a class discussion of each question. Encourage further thought by asking additional questions: *What color is the smell? What does it make you feel inside? What do you hear when you smell that odor? What does that odor taste like?* Solicit a variety of comparisons and list them on the board.

Give students ten or fifteen minutes to complete "What Is That Smell I Feel?" As they work, offer guidance, answer questions, and make suggestions.

EPISODE 4.2. Lead a class discussion of the students' answers. Begin by asking students to read aloud the sentence they wrote for Question 5. Comment on any effective details and figurative language students have used in their culminating sentence to encourage them and reinforce their achievements. Ask the class to help revise any sentences that need improvement. Once all the sentences have been read, ask for volunteers to read the comparisons they wrote for Question 4 and highlight effective ones. Finally, discuss their answers to Questions 2 and 3. Point out particularly effective descriptions and discuss why they are distinctive and memorable.

EPISODE 4.3. Reinforce the skills you've introduced by giving students, in pairs or trios or perhaps on their own this time, a second, different Scratch'n'Sniff sticker and a new activity sheet. Repeat the procedures, adjusting your instruction to scaffold the students' ability to describe odors in vivid ways.

EPISODE 4.4. Have students expand on the strategies they have learned by describing in writing a location in which odors are an important part of the experience: ethnic restaurants, a locker room, the school cafeteria, the beach, a dumpster, a new car, a kitchen, a candy store, an alley, a bakery, a laundry room, a creek bed, a feed store, a pine forest, factories making specific products (paint, cars, paper products, insect repellants, and so on). Depending on their readiness to take on an independent project of this sort, you might include various types of scaffolds to help them connect what they have learned in the previous activities to what they will write on their own. You might, for instance, have the class describe a place within the school that has a distinctive smell, such as the art room, a locker room, a chemistry lab, or if you're especially adventure-some, a lavatory. Lead a discussion of the smells in this location and how they could be described. Then, using a chalkboard, overhead projector, or document camera, help students take their observations and ideas and formulate them into a description of the site and its olfactory impressions.

Depending on how much time you have, you might then have small groups of students describe a second school location without your explicit leadership. Students could brainstorm smells, collaborate on writing a description of the place, exchange papers with another group and receive feedback, and then write a final version to turn in. These descriptions could be collected to create an "Olfactory Guide to [Your School]."

At this point, students may be ready to produce a piece of writing individually that vividly evokes the smells present in a place outside the school.

Stage 5. Generating a Topic

Now that students have spent a number of days learning how to observe closely and describe specific sensory details using figurative language, they are ready to start using both visual and olfactory details to make their personal experience narrative come alive.

EPISODE 5.1. Give students the same assignment you used for your preliminary assessment of their narrative writing proficiency:

Write about a personal experience and its consequences that had an impact on you or someone you know. Be as specific as you can in describing the event and its consequences or impact. Try to write so that a reader will see what you saw and feel what you felt.

Repeating this open-ended assignment lets you contrast their original narratives with the ones they produce now and thus assess the effects of your instruction so far. Presumably, their use of detail will have improved to the point where they can undertake new kinds of writing—in this case, a narrative rather than a description—that employ the same procedures.

If students have trouble finding topics to write about, brainstorm story ideas. Thinking aloud, come up with a list of five or six ideas, assess them, and narrow the possibilities to one that meets the criteria for the assignment. Of course, matters of school propriety need to be considered. Then ask a series of questions to prompt their thinking, encouraging them to generate at least one idea for each question.

1. Remember a time when you felt really happy about something or someone. What happened that made you feel so happy?

2. Recall a time when you felt very sad about something or someone. What happened that made you feel so sad?

3. Think about the most important person in your life. What happened that made you realize how important this person is to you?

4. Remember a time when you experienced an important ritual or event that was a critical moment in your life. Why was it so important?

5. Remember a time in your life when you worked hard to accomplish something and you were able to do it. What happened? How did you accomplish your goal?

6. Recall an occasion when you worked hard to accomplish or achieve something and fell short. What happened? How did things go wrong?

7. Think of a time when you were faced with a difficult decision. What happened? Did you make the right decision? Why or why not?

8. Recall a time in your life when you had to make an ethical or moral choice. What was the choice? Did you do the right thing?

9. Consider an occasion when you had to stand up for yourself or others in the face of danger. How did you act in this situation?

10. Remember a time in your life when you were really frightened or scared. What happened? Were you able to overcome your fear? If so, how? If not, why not?

EPISODE 5.2.   Have students, in pairs or small groups, present their topic ideas to and get feedback from their partner or fellow group members. They can use the following questions as a guide:

1. Which ideas seem most interesting, exciting, or compelling as the basis for a personal experience narrative?

2. Which ideas best lend themselves to incorporating sensory detail?

3. Are any of the topics inappropriate for school writing?

4. Which idea do you think the writer should write about? Why?

You could also ask the pairs or groups to tell the whole class which topics they think would be the best one to write about and why. Hearing what other students are doing and thinking helps students refine their ideas.

Stage 6. Generating Task-Specific Evaluation Criteria

By evaluating stories written by other students before they begin writing their own, students develop discrimination they can apply to their work. They might also create a checklist of what needs to be included. There is no "best" place for this step, but it's a critical element of any writing instruction. The right place to include it is a judgment call. In this sequence the detail activities take several days, and generating criteria works well just before students begin writing.

EPISODE 6.1. Have students, in small groups, analyze and discuss the narratives in Figures 1–1, 1–2, and 1–4, ranking the essays from best to worst. ("The Hit" is usually considered the best, "Car Wash," second, and "Scary Encounter," the weakest.) Then ask them to list the qualities or features that distinguish stronger from weaker personal experience narratives.

Figure 1–4. Personal Experience Essay: "The Hit"

As I stepped up to the plate, I could hear the quiet cheers of the crowd in back of me. I laid down my bat on the just swept plate. I could feel my palms begin to sweat as the night air blew a gust of wind past my body. I reached down and picked up some dirt, and as I did, I could feel the heat from the large lights of the ballpark.

I stood up and took a step back from the plate to take a couple of practice swings. My muscles felt tight but began to loosen up as I swung the bat. Finally, the umpire said, "Okay, let's play ball!"

I felt my adrenalin pump through my body. I knew that I had to hit a home run because it was the ninth inning with two outs against us, and we had our worst hitter coming up after me. I laid the bat on my shoulder very gently and took a deep breath while waiting for the pitcher to go into his windup. Finally, the pitcher nodded his head to show he agreed with the signal from the catcher, and he leaned back into his windup. To me he looked almost motionless until he reached forward and released the ball into its swirling orbit. The ball came so fast that it almost caught me off guard. I knew if I waited any longer the ball would go whirling past me, and I would miss a perfect pitch. So I swung the bat around with all my might and hoped that I would make contact. I knew that I really hit the ball because I heard a cracking

(continues)

Figure 1–4. Personal Experience Essay: "The Hit" (*continued*)

noise and then I felt a tingling sensation running from my fingers up to my forearm.

At first I could not see the ball in the night sky so I almost thought that I had hit it out of bounds. Yet I heard the crowd cheering so I knew the ball must still be flying in the air. Then I spotted it sailing way up in the sky.

I dropped my bat and ran while at the same time keeping an eye on the ball. I rounded first still running my hardest. Half way to second I dropped my head and put all my might into it because I saw the ball drop right in front of the left fielder's feet. I knew I had to get all the way home. I rounded second. The third base coach signaled for me to stop at third, but I knew that I could make it. I rounded third at full steam, took a wide turn, and headed for home. I saw the catcher getting ready to catch the ball so I took a diving leap, stretching my muscles to touch home plate.

I hit the ground with a thump and began to slide. I could not see anything through all the dust. I reached for the plate and looked up at the umpire. He stood there very still, and then both arms flung to the side as he called me "Safe!"

EPISODE 6.2.   Lead a class discussion of group findings and list the features of a high-quality personal experience narrative on the board. Typical features include:

1. The personal experience is sharply focused with a strong impact—the details create an overall impression.

2. The narrative contains a variety of specific, concrete sensory details and includes figurative language (simile, metaphor, personification, etc.).

3. When appropriate, the narrative uses dialogue effectively.

4. The details and dialogue contribute to the overall impression; the writer has selected and arranged details for effect.

5. The writer uses sentence structure, word choice, vocabulary, and other aspects of language that are suitable for the narrator and situation.

EPISODE 6.3. If additional work seems warranted, have small groups come up with ideas for improving one of the narratives they have evaluated and lead a class discussion of those ideas. Students might also revise the story in small groups or on their own so that they get experience in adding appropriate details to narratives.

Stage 7. Language Lesson: Playing with Participial Phrases

A minilesson on sentence structure helps students make their narratives more vivid by consciously varying their syntax when relating events. Recognizing and using introductory participial phrases is one useful structure. (You may identify other possibilities more appropriate for your students.)

EPISODE 7.1. Define *participle*. A *participle* is a verb form that has the function either of a verb used as part of the predicate or of an adjective. The present participle always ends in *-ing*; the past participle of most regular verbs ends in *-ed* or *-en*. For example:

Present participle, part of predicate: I am *cooking* a casserole for dinner.

Past participle, part of predicate: I have *cooked* a casserole for dinner.

A participle can also be an adjective, often appearing as the first word in an adjectival phrase that describes the subject of a sentence. For example:

Present participial phrase: *Cooking all day*, I prepared a lovely meal.

Past participial phrase: *Cooked too long*, the brownies were rather crisp.

Participial phrases are an interesting way to vary sentence structure. They can also result in comical sentences when they are intended to modify one noun but instead modify another. Here's a memorable sentence written by one of our students: "Crashing into the rocks, the gulls flew above the waves." The participial phrase is *crashing into the rocks*. Presumably, the author meant to say that the waves were crashing into the rocks as the gulls flew overhead. However, as written, the sentence says that the gulls were crashing into the rocks. Ouch.

EPISODE 7.2. To help students construct sentences that open with a participial phrase, give them pairs of brief sentences that they combine into one sentence in which the opening phrase begins with a present or past participle.

Here are two brief sentences that could be combined into one by converting one of the sentences into a participial phrase:

Todd drove home from work one day.

Todd saw something he had never seen before.

Ask, "What is the present participial form of *drove*?" If students don't say *driving*, follow up with, "How could you take the first sentence and make it into a participial phrase that modifies the second sentence?" Eventually you should arrive at, *Driving home from work one day, Todd saw something he had never seen before.*

Then model the same process using a past participial phrase to combine these sentences:

I was blinded by the light. I didn't see the train coming.

EPISODE 7.3. Prompt students to realize how easily participial structures can modify an unintended noun by having them complete an exercise like the one in Figure 1–5.

EPISODE 7.4. Students are now ready to practice combining pairs of sentences into a single sentence that opens with a participial phrase (see the exercise in Figure 1–6). It doesn't matter whether they use a past or present participle, as long as the phrase modifies the intended noun.

Stage 8. Drafting the Narratives

Have students write a draft of their personal experience narrative. Decide whether they do so in class or as homework and how long

Figure 1–5. Participial Phrase or Dangling Participle?

The following sentences open with either a past or present participial phrase. Each modifies a noun in the main clause of the sentence. Work with a partner to tell which noun it modifies, and then decide whether it modifies the noun that the author intended or not. Rewrite any sentence in which you think the phrase modifies the wrong noun.

1. Blasted by the dynamite, the coal miners opened up a new mine shaft in the mountain.

2. Coming around the corner, I saw my path blocked by a dumpster on the sidewalk.

3. Forgotten by everyone, poor little Joey was left behind at the field trip to the museum.

4. Stuffing food into my mouth, my mother told me to hurry up and finish my dinner.

5. Believing that crime does not pay, the judge ordered the ice cream truck thief to spend the rest of his life in jail.

6. Blown over by the tornado, the townspeople rebuilt the court house.

7. Buried under five feet of snow, we used shovels to uncover my car.

8. Throwing right-handed, Lefty McDougle's spear landed right next to the bull's eye and hit his eyebrow.

9. Piled high on my desk, the papers made it hard for me to work.

10. Taking an extra fifty dollars, the bank was unaware of my large withdrawal.

before the draft is due. Encourage them to include the three aspects of writing emphasized in the instruction: clear descriptive details; sensory images, including those related to smell; and sentences introduced by participial phrases.

Figure 1–6. Sentence Combining Exercise—Participial Phrases

Each item below contains two sentences. Combine them into one sentence that opens with either a past or present participial phrase. Make sure the phrase modifies the word you intend it to describe.

1. Bigby Hinds was getting hungry. Bigby decided to grab a bite to eat.

2. Bigby walked down the street. Bigby was looking for a restaurant.

3. Dinah Thirst was late for work at the onion-processing plant. Dinah was driving a bit too fast.

4. Dinah saw Bigby walking down the sidewalk. Dinah wondered why Bigby didn't appear to have a job.

5. Bigby was getting hungrier by the moment. Bigby caught a whiff of Dinah's onion-scented car.

6. Bigby was plagued by a recent operation to his nasal passages. Bigby couldn't tell the difference between Dinah's car and an onion burger.

7. Dinah swerved to avoid a possum. Dinah turned the wheel of her car frantically.

8. Bigby strongly resembled a possum. Bigby didn't smell so good either.

9. Bigby smelled neither good nor well. Bigby was considering getting a rhinoscopy and taking a shower.

10. Dinah thought this was a splendid idea. Dinah drove more carefully to the onion-processing plant with a clothespin on her nose.

Stage 9. Responding to Drafts

EPISODE 9.1. Have students, in groups of three or four, use the features of a successful personal experience narrative they developed in class to evaluate one another's narratives and suggest revisions. Have each group do the following for each person's narrative:

1. Tell the writer one thing that he or she did well. What is the most effective feature or aspect of the narrative?

2. Tell the writer one thing that could be improved. What feature is missing or weak in the narrative?

3. Suggest one thing the writer could do to improve the weak part of the narrative.

Then have each student in the group read the other group members' essays silently and mark any errors in spelling, punctuation, and grammar for possible correction.

EPISODE 9.2. Ask the students to revise their drafts in light of the feedback they have received and what they have learned by critiquing their classmates' papers.

EPISODE 9.3. Have the students, in small groups, read their finished narratives aloud. Each group might also select one personal experience essay to read aloud to the class. To evaluate the essays, refer to the criteria that the students generated when evaluating the three sample narratives. In general, evaluate the students on what they've been taught in the instruction leading directly to the writing, rather than hypercorrecting by marking every error. Students often experience "cognitive overload" when given too much feedback on too many aspects of writing. The consensus from research is that focused feedback—feedback centered on specific matters that have been recently taught—is far more beneficial to student writers than comprehensive feedback they may find overwhelming (Hillocks 1986).

Extensions

1. Have students, in small groups, turn one narrative (or a combination of narratives) into a skit, a filmed short play, a storyboard, an animated short feature, or whatever means of dramatization they come up with, and perform it for or present it to the class.

2. Have students write personal experience narratives that relate to the themes they are studying in the literature they are reading: for example, coming of age,

responsibility, adolescent relationships, conflict with authority (see www.coe.uga.edu/~smago/VirtualLibrary/ UnitOutlines.htm, and Smagorinsky 2008).

3. Have students write a personal experience narrative on their blog and get feedback from visitors. This more public presentation moves student writing outside the classroom into wider social spaces.

4. Have students enter their narrative in a writing competition, submit it to a print publication such as *Merlyn's Pen* or NCTE's *Teen Ink*, or post it online.

Summing Up

These lessons scaffold students' progress through a sequence of activities in which they learn specific procedures and strategies for producing a personal narrative. They receive support from both you and their peers at each stage of the process, and you monitor their learning and determine whether or not additional activities are necessary before moving forward. Your judgment is an important factor throughout the instruction, but the students are active participants in the classroom. Through careful design and preparation—and wise consideration of the degree to which students have grasped procedures for producing engaging personal narratives—you play a critical if at times hidden role in the students' development as writers.

Questions for Reflection

1. Are there any personal narrative topics that would be off limits to your student writers? Which ones, and why?

2. Can excessive details derail a narrative's momentum? How do you address this problem?

3. Would you encourage or discourage writing by students from immigrant families that includes non-English phrases?

4. How can technology help students write personal narratives?

5. Is it appropriate to include genres such as art and music in personal narratives? Why or why not?

6. Can you incorporate personal narrative instruction into your grade level's language and literature curriculum?

7. How can instruction in personal narrative writing help prepare your students to take standardized tests?

8. How do you know when a student has written a good personal narrative? What determines the quality of the topic, the story arc, the characters, the details, the descriptive language, the dialogue, and so on?

Teaching Personal Narratives Within a Thematic Unit of Instruction

There are times when writing is taught as an end in itself, as in the lessons in Chapter 1. Often, however, students write in the context of other areas of the curriculum. Many teachers, for instance, embed their instruction in grammar and syntax in students' writing (see Weaver 1996). Writing may also be taught as a way to think about literature, as a way to report research, and so on.

In much of our other work, we advocate embedding writing instruction in the English curriculum as a whole. We believe the English curriculum can be fruitfully organized as a related series of explorations of themes, reading strategies, genres and archetypes, literary periods, philosophical movements, geographic regions, and the works of specific authors (Hillocks et al. 1971; Smagorinsky 2008).

The junior year American literature curriculum, for instance, might address the idea of the American dream in eight or ten units (four or five a semester), each covering four to six weeks, formed around such topics as the Puritan ethic, protest literature, materialism and success, progress and technology, social responsibility, the individual and society, satire, gender roles, justice, frontier literature, changing times, the banality of evil, the family, immigration, the frontier, propaganda, discrimination, cultural conflict, the Harlem renaissance, Transcendentalism, authors of Mississippi, and the poems of Emily Dickinson. This approach departs from the conventional way of teaching American literature in chronological order. It allows you to cluster works from specific literary periods that share themes and other key motifs. At www.coe.uga .edu/~smago/VirtualLibrary/Unit_Outlines.htm there is a large (and ever-growing) collection of conceptual unit ideas, often accompanied by specific lesson plans. Organizing instruction around a concept helps students track an idea through a series of texts, each leading to a better understanding of both the previous one and the next one.

Personal narratives can be part of any conceptual instructional unit, whatever the organizational category. For example:

- *Themes*. In a unit on *the family*, students could write personal narratives about events from family life that reveal relationships (not all of them positive) fostered at home.

- *Genres or archetypes*. In a unit on *the journey*, students could relate a personal journey they have taken in which they have experienced challenges typical to this genre, such as beasts or monsters that must be overcome, partners or mentors who accompany the traveler, barrier crossings, trials endured along the way, rites of initiation and other rituals, and the return to and reintegration with the community.

- *Reading strategies*. In a unit on *understanding point of view*, students could write a personal narrative and then retell it from the perspective of different speakers.

- *Literary periods*. During a study of *the Jazz Age*, students could write narratives that illustrate the sort of rebellion against established values that characterized the period.

- *Movements*. Students could produce narratives related to the environmental conservation practices of the *Transcendentalists*.

- *Regions.* Students could produce personal narratives in which the setting is central to the emotions and experiences related, such as a unit on *a sense of place* or the *authors of the Great Lakes region.*

- *Particular authors.* When studying *the works of Edgar Allen Poe,* students could write a personal narrative in which they parody Poe's style.

This chapter uses personal narratives in the context of a unit focused on a sense of place. The region in which a person is born and raised engenders visual, emotional, experiential, ritualistic, and relational images that establish a strong sense of grounding and belonging. The unit can include reading and responding to memoir (e.g., Sandra Cisneros' *House on Mango Street*), song (e.g., Alan Jackson's "Chattahoochee"), fiction (e.g., Leslie Marmon Silko's *Ceremony*), autobiography (e.g., Amy Blackmarr's *House of Steps: Adventures of a Southerner in Kansas*), poetry (e.g., Walt Whitman's "I Hear America Singing"), a collection of impressions (e.g., Studs Terkel's *Chicago*), nonfiction (e.g., Washington Irving's *A Tour on the Prairie*), film (e.g., *A River Runs Through It*), art (e.g., the Alaskan landscape paintings of James Buncak; see http://picturealaska.com/JamesBuncak.htm), and other texts that help students understand how a place influences one's personality, ideology, and other aspects of human development.

Students could write about their own experiences as a prereading activity to prepare them for the kinds of issues they will encounter in the texts they will read. Writing about those experiences helps students develop the "cognitive map" psychologists have found useful in learning new information. Using their own experiences as a framework for the sorts of textual structures, concepts, themes, and other emphases of the unit, students more readily understand the ideas of the texts they will then read. In turn, the students' reading of the texts enhances their understanding of their own experiences. Their writing and reading are well integrated in mutually informative ways.

When writing instruction is accompanied by instruction in some relevant aspect of language usage, the three traditional strands of the curriculum are woven together to produce rich learning experiences. Further, engagement with and perhaps production of digital texts and other products of new and emerging twenty-first-century technologies can provide texture and variety. Broadening the texts available to students increases their ability and desire to participate in teaching and learning.

Simply assigning writing related to unit themes and concepts, however, is insufficient. You need to help students develop their writing by teaching them strategies for producing the features that bring their narratives to life. Teaching students procedures for writing personal narratives then becomes a central dimension of the unit's instruction, one that both helps them with their writing during the unit (and beyond) and helps them understand how the authors they study have crafted their own texts.

The lessons in this chapter were taught in the classroom of Joanna Anglin, of Rockdale Career Academy (RCA), in Conyers, Georgia. RCA is a charter school emphasizing career, technical, workforce, and academic preparation for students in a large, diverse county outside Atlanta. It enrolls over 1,200 students who concentrate on one of eighteen technical "majors" and simultaneously have access to a variety of internship, apprenticeship, and industry credentialing experiences that give their education both relevance and application. Joanna, while new to this school, has taught in this district for about a decade. In addition to having begun her doctoral studies at The University of Georgia, she was named the 2011 recipient of the Georgia Council of Teachers of English State Teacher of the Year award. Joanna says about her instruction:

> In implementing these strategies, I found that my students responded positively to the variety of the activities—listening to songs about Georgia; describing images from various regions in Georgia; and constructing phrases about smells, tastes, or sights that they normally overlook. Having to create descriptive phrases challenged their skills in both observation and vocabulary. However, the progression of the activities helped the students craft interesting and meaningful compositions.

The activities that follow help young writers convey the sensory detail and emotional resonance related to a place. Throughout the sequence, the students discuss their work with their classmates as they prewrite, draft, revise with attention to particular features, and develop final versions of their narratives. This process also contributes to their understanding of the published texts they read during the unit. Because class times vary from school to school, the activities specify time rather than days or class periods required.

Task Analysis

The features of personal narratives identified in Chapter 1 remain in play when writing narratives related to a sense of place: Students should include details in their writing and provide sensory images associated with the setting. Since that setting is a place of special significance, they should also reveal their emotional ties to the setting.

Stage 1. Assessing What Students Know About Narrative

EPISODE 1.1. Use the following prompt to find out what students do and do not know about the features of personal narratives and how to produce them:

> Write about a personal experience in a place of significance to you. Tell your story so that it is clear why this place is important to your experiences. Make sure that your readers will be able to see, hear, smell, touch, and taste the environment and experience your emotions about the place along with you. Be as specific as you can in describing the event and its consequences or impact.

Give students about forty-five minutes to write their narratives (time may vary depending on the students' age and writing development).

EPISODE 1.2. Use these narratives to decide what to emphasize in your instruction. Typically, students will have trouble providing details that help readers empathize. Their responses may be a single paragraph that begins with an awkward introductory sentence, includes few if any descriptive sensory details, and does not convey the emotional importance of the location. The instruction that follows teaches students procedures for incorporating detail and emotional resonance into their narrative writing.

Stage 2. Gateway Activity: Promoting Attention to Detail

One way to introduce both the writing and the unit is to have the students inductively identify features they find particularly evocative in images that capture the essence of a place. The website www .coe.uga.edu/~smago/VirtualLibrary/Unit_Outlines.htm#USStates contains links to the literature, music, images, and tastes of the fifty United States. Thousands of stock photos of each state are also available at www.allposters.com, www.fotosearch.com, and http:// images.google.com. The activity here focuses on the state of New Jersey but can be easily adapted to any state or region.

New Jersey has a reputation for being highly industrialized and is infamous for its urban centers of considerable blight. Anyone who has driven along its turnpike can attest to the abundance of belching factory smokestacks that rise above its cities, especially in the northern part of the state, and the fetid odors they emit, which penetrate tightly shut car windows and make passengers yearn, quite literally, for greener pastures. Yet New Jersey also has an extensive ocean shore that attracts millions of people each summer; vast pine barrens that extend across the southern part of the state; a western border along the beautiful Delaware River; northern mountain ranges that include scenic lakes; affluent suburbs of both Philadelphia and New York City; the stately campus of Princeton University and other colleges; and other assets. They also grow a heck of a tomato in New Jersey, and the Jersey Devil purportedly haunts the pine barrens. Authors who have written about the state explain how its physical, cultural, and social environment helped shape the character of the people who live there.

EPISODE 2.1. This activity is based on various New Jersey images: specific cities or counties; geographic areas such as the Jersey shore, the Delaware River Valley, or the pine barrens; human constructions such as the Atlantic City boardwalk or the sights available at the New Jersey Festival of Ballooning; historical sites such as the state's many Revolutionary War battlefields; or other features of interest and importance in shaping the culture of the state. Depending on the resources available in your school and classroom, students could use the Internet to find their own images, or you could identify an appropriate set and convert them to overheads, handouts, or a slideshow to use in class. The images should include both beautiful and noteworthy, and devastated, shameful, and embarrassing attributes. Since promotional photos and posters typically focus on the positive, negative aspects may need to be approached from the perspective of what the positive images overlook or avoid.

Have students, in small groups, spend thirty minutes (or more, depending on the number of images viewed, the age and maturity of the students, and other pertinent factors) examining these images and drawing conclusions about what they reveal about the state. In their analysis, they could focus on such questions as:

1. What sights, sounds, smells, tastes, and senses of touch do the pictures portray or suggest?

2. What emotions are suggested by these images?

3. What overall sense of place emerges from the images and emotions depicted and suggested in the pictures?

4. What stories about personal experiences would you associate with the places in these pictures?

Each student should keep a record, using a graphic organizer similar to Figure 2–1, of the images, emotions, sense of place, and associated personal narratives.

EPISODE 2.2. Lead a whole-class discussion of the small-group findings. Ask each group to report its observations, inferences, and conclusions. For the Jersey Shore, for example, students might identify *sights* such as seagulls, driftwood, the ocean, sunbathers, ships at sea, swimmers, kite flyers, lifeguards in their towers, and refreshment stands. *Sounds* could include the calls of shore birds, the crashing of waves, the shrieks of children, the whistling of a carousel

Figure 2–1. Senses Portrayed or Suggested in Pictures and the
Emotions They Trigger

	PLACE 1	PLACE 2	PLACE 3	PLACE 4	PLACE 5	PLACE 6	PLACE 7	PLACE 8
Sights								
Sounds								
Tastes								
Smells								
Touch								
Emotions								
Sense of Place								
Associated Personal Narratives								

calliope, and the like. *Tastes* would include the ocean salt in the air, the occasional grains of sand inhaled, a first kiss, saltwater taffy, food from vendors or cookouts, and so on. Students might identify *smells* such as the salty air, the cotton candy from the food stands, the suntan lotion on people's bodies, seaweed and other ocean effluvium washed up on shore, and other odors. Through their sense of *touch* students could experience the hot sand on their feet, the burn from a jellyfish accidentally stepped upon, the wind blowing in from the ocean, the splintery wood of the boardwalk, the gritty sensation of sand in their shoes, and so on. They might associate *emotions* of anticipation, happiness, disappointment, exhilaration, shame, relief, and other feelings related to *personal narratives* of summertime romance, school vacations, adventures with friends, dumpster diving, and other memorable occurrences related to trips to special and evocative places.

Other positive images students might identify include scenes from the Delaware Water Gap, the pine barrens, particular towns and cities, or attractions such as the state aquarium. Negative images could include organized crime (including the fictional cable TV drama *The Sopranos*), pollution from factories, congested roadways, endless construction and road repair, the repellant people on the TV reality shows *Housewives of New Jersey* and *Jersey Shore*, strip malls, and other images generally not featured in promotional photographs and posters.

Up to now you'll have done a relatively small amount of talking in class, limiting your contribution to giving directions, eavesdropping on discussions, and redirecting students who stray off task. Students have examined the images, talked in their groups about their observations and inferences related to the senses and emotions the images evoked, charted their analysis on a graphic organizer, reported their findings to the class, and commented on one another's findings. In other words, once in class, the students do the majority of the work and the talking. Below, Joanna describes how she scaffolded her students' ability to phrase their observations in captivating language:

> My students found this activity the most enjoyable but the most difficult. While they could tell me what emotions were evoked

by the images that I provided of Georgia—a baseball stadium on a sunny summer day, a moss-covered driveway in Savannah, a beach scene from coastal Georgia—they had more difficulty providing phrases capturing the five senses. I had to provide examples and coach them through the process to create longer descriptive phrases beyond one-word answers such as *wet, salty,* or *hot.* However, after the small groups shared their descriptors and helped one another expand on them, they were able to produce longer phrases and even some sentences. My students particularly enjoyed creating sentences describing negative images of their beloved city—"the hairy rat picks through the rotting garbage that smells like a dirty diaper" or "the bitter car exhaust looms over glass from broken windows."

Her remarks illustrate two key contributions to students' learning: a sensitivity to what they need to understand better in order to work effectively, and the ability to provide appropriate levels of support.

Stage 3. Initial Drafting

The instruction in Stage 1 and Stage 2 has emphasized *ideas* rather than *form.* One common formula for writing narratives stresses that stories have a beginning, middle, and end. In reality, however, some pretty famous stories start in the middle (e.g., Homer's *The Odyssey,* Virgil's *Aeneid,* Milton's *Paradise Lost*) or are told in reverse order (e.g., Pinter's *Betrayal* and the *Seinfeld* episode based on it, Amis' *Time's Arrow,* the anime television series *Touka Gettan*) or involve flashbacks and flashforwards (e.g., the television series *Lost,* Spark's *The Prime of Miss Jean Brodie*) or have no clear ending (e.g., many Arabian Nights tales, many Native American stories) or otherwise violate this truism. Therefore this sequence begins with content and assumes that form will follow from function.

You can proceed in one of two ways. If your students are relatively mature and already know a lot about writing personal narratives, you might have them start right in writing. If your students are less experienced writers they might, as an intermediate step, return to their small groups and discuss potential places and stories.

We advocate departing from the conventional wisdom that *people learn to write by writing*. We believe *people learn to write not only by writing but by talking about writing throughout the process*. Small groups are key, because they allow free-spirited discussion, risk taking, and immediate critical feedback. The following sequence helps prepare relatively young writers whose narrative writing is not yet well refined for the demands of writing personal narratives.

EPISODE 3.1. Have students, in small groups, explore possible places and stories and get feedback on how to proceed. Students may read, listen to, and view personal narratives of published authors, photographers, artists, songwriters, and directors as they consider the importance of a sense of place and the role of one particular place in how they have grown as a person and experienced that growth emotionally.

EPISODE 3.2. When each student has settled on a topic and setting for a personal narrative, give everyone an assignment like that in Figure 2–2. How much class time you dedicate to this part of the activity depends on your timetable, students' ability to work outside class, your school's policies regarding homework, and numerous other factors. In response to this assignment, Joanna's eleventh-grade student Leigh produced the rough draft reproduced in Figure 2–3.

Figure 2–2. Instructions for Writing a Personal Narrative

Write a personal narrative set in a place of special importance to you. Your story may follow any structure that suits your purposes. As you write, try to include details about the sights, smells, tastes, touches, and sounds that characterize the place and that contribute to your story. Don't get hung up on details for now. You will have opportunities to revise your writing later, and you will participate in activities in class that help you generate those sensory images. Also, try to verbalize the feelings you associate with both your story and the place in which you set it. Don't get bogged down with your emotional account, though, because you will have opportunities to work on this part of your story later too.

Figure 2–3. Leigh's Rough Draft

Walking past the talk oak tree, luke-warm tears begin to fall. I know I shouldn't cry but images of you fill my mind. I continue walking until I find the spot. Once there I sit, and [crossout] start thinking about happy thoughts. All the memories shared, laughs giggled and the little simple smiles we gave to each other. I know you're smiling now so with that I begin to speak. I say "Hello" and tell you "that I miss you" but all [crossout] I hear is silence. The silence that fills my mind and voids my thoughts but before I fully lose myself [crossout] I return back to my one sided conversation. I tell you about school and how I hope you're proud of me, but still no answer. [crossout] I [crossout] search for answers from within. The only response I seek from myself is that I suppose no matter what I do you'd want your little sunshine to be happy and fulfill her dreams with that in mind, I truly hope to never let you down. After seeking my [crossout] answers I look around to see no-one [crossout] their. just empty space. It seems to be such a lonely place even though its filled with so many soulful individuals. I begin to stand but before I go I sing to you "you are my sunshine" so you never forget that I'm always thinking of you. I place flowers upon your [crossout] grave, look up to the sky and simply say I love you. I'll be back soon even though I know you're always watching. I take those steps, then drive away.

Students' initial drafts are the material to which, following instruction, they will add sensory detail and emotional quality. In Chapter 1, students were taught about sensory detail instruction before writing their drafts. There is no fixed recipe for sequencing these activities. If your students produce better writing when they learn procedures for generating detail before drafting, adjust your instructional sequence accordingly.

Stage 4. Small-Group Activities on Developing Sensory Detail

In the unit's initial activity, students considered the five senses and how they contribute to experiencing a sense of place. This introductory emphasis on sensory detail provides ideas and material students can apply to subsequent drafts of their narratives. How much attention you give to sensory detail depends on the level at which your students are presently writing and how much time you have for specific lessons on each of the five senses. The episodes below assume you have a great deal of time and can draw students' attention to each of the five senses individually. The goal of each activity is for students to consider both mundane and exceptional sensory impressions and how they could be described. You can pick and choose from them according to your needs. You can, of course, gather materials ahead of time, but "found" materials that students already have in their possession or that are available in the classroom are a shortcut when you are pressed for time. The descriptions below include suggestions for using found materials.

EPISODE 4.1. Present a lesson on describing visual details. Give an example like the following:

> The simplest description is often how things appear to the eye. A writer might say, for instance, "The wind blew my hair in my eyes," but the image lacks detail. A more vivid description might be: "The breeze picked up speed. My hair blew wildly, slapping my face. Bits of debris pelted my eyes and blurred my vision. Colors and shapes melted into one another."

Ask students, in groups of three to five, to find imaginative ways to describe seemingly ordinary things. You might say:

- "Identify a place with which you are all familiar: a school gym, a creek bed, a Laundromat, a street corner, a pond, an empty lot, a specific restaurant, or other location."

- "List the sights that you might see in this place."

- "Discuss how you might describe each sight in more vivid detail, and write down the best phrasings you come up with."

- "Share your phrasings with the class, and critique one another's word choices and level of detail."

EPISODE 4.2.   Present a lesson on describing sounds. Give an example like the following:

> Most places are characterized by sounds, and writers often include them in their descriptions. A writer might say, for example, "The bell rang." This statement lacks detail. A more vivid description might be: "The shrill shriek of the bell ending another class echoed in my ears as I trudged off to lunch."

Ask students, in groups of three to five, to think of ways in which to describe sounds imaginatively and with detail. You might say:

- "Identify a place with which you are all familiar: a train stop, a ballpark, a bowling alley, a video arcade, an orchard, or other location."

- "List the sounds you might hear in this place."

- "Discuss how you might describe each sound in more vivid detail, and write down the best phrasings you come up with."

- "Share your phrasings with the class, and critique one another's word choices and level of detail."

EPISODE 4.3.   Present a lesson on describing the sense of taste. Give an example like the following:

> Often places have tastes associated with them. For example, a writer might say, "The coffee in the diner tasted bitter." A more vivid description might be: "I lifted the coffee cup to my lips. As the coffee slid into my mouth, it bit into my tongue like a rattlesnake pouncing on a mouse."

Ask students, in groups of three to five, to think of ways to describe taste so that readers can experience the sensation viscerally. You might say:

- "List a number of things that you eat or otherwise chew or touch with your tongue. For example, some people chew on pencils, erasers, gum, fingernails, and other assorted inedible materials (although health risks are involved!)."

- "For the items you select, describe in simple language how they taste—the chocolate cream pie tasted velvety, the stale gum was leathery and too sweet, and so on."

- "Discuss how you might describe each taste in more vivid detail, and write down the best phrasings you come up with."

- "Share your phrasings with the class, and critique one another's word choices and level of detail."

EPISODE 4.4.   Present a lesson on describing tactile sensations. Give an example like the following:

> Most places and things have distinctive physical sensations associated with them, and writers often include them in their descriptions. For example, a writer might say, "The pink bunny suit was furry." You could, however, come up with a more vivid description: "I stroked the fur of the pink bunny suit, the cheap fibers feeling like the hair of an ancient woolly mammoth just exhumed from a melting glacier."

Ask students, in groups of three to five, to come up with vivid ways to describe how ordinary objects feel. You might say:

- "In your classroom or among your belongings, find things that provide tactile sensations: items from your purse or wallet, implements such as pens or binders, the classroom walls, articles of clothing, and so on."

- "Run your fingers over each item and describe it as clearly as possible."

- "Discuss how you might describe each item's texture in more vivid detail, and write down the best phrasings you come up with."

- "Share your phrasings with the class, and critique one another's word choices and level of detail."

EPISODE 4.5. Present a lesson on describing smells. Give an example like the following:

> Writers often describe how something smells. For example, a writer might say, "My grandpa's overcoat smelled musty and stale." However, that description could be expanded and made more vivid: "As my grandad hugged me, my nose encountered a hazy swamp in which a truck carrying toxic waste had crashed into a vat of Eau de Locker Room perfume."

Ask students, in groups of three to five, to think of ways in which to describe smells imaginatively and with detail. You might say:

- "In your classroom or among your belongings, find things that give off an intriguing odor: items from your purse or wallet, the fabric in the clothing you're wearing, something in your backpack, the pencil sharpener, and so on."

- "Sniff each item and describe the smells as clearly as possible."

- "Discuss how you might describe each item's aroma in more vivid detail, and write down the best phrasings you come up with."

- "Share your phrasings with the class, and critique one another's word choices and level of detail."

Below, Joanna describes using these exercises in her classroom:

> When I implemented these activities in my classroom, I found that certain senses provided more difficulty than others. Students found describing the sense of taste almost impossible. As I monitored their discussions, students asked questions like, "What does a book bag taste like?" I simple smiled, shrugged, and asked them, "What do *you* think it tastes like?" Many students resorted to actually tasting items like these, but they found that did not help much. The problem was they hadn't had to describe the sense of taste before. However, by the end of the five lessons, all the students experienced some success with describing items and with the depth of their descriptions. This ability was evident when they applied this skill during their revisions.

Joanna didn't answer the students' questions directly, instead encouraging them to figure things out on their own. Had this method of scaffolding not produced results, she might have provided something more explicit, perhaps a *think-aloud* demonstrating the process of generating vivid descriptions. Backup scaffolding should always be part of your repertoire when teaching students how to develop new and challenging ways of expressing themselves.

Stage 5. Applying Sensory Detail to Draft Narratives

Peer review is a critical phase of the highly social writing process we advocate throughout this series of books. Peer review provides two important benefits: (1) the students get immediate feedback on their writing and have an opportunity to make revisions before submitting it for formal evaluation, and (2) students' critiques of their peers' writing help them develop their own writing fluency.

Some educators criticize peer review as "the blind leading the blind"; the way they see it, students are providing feedback without having developed the expertise and judgment necessary for their advice to be of value. From a developmental standpoint, however, providing a critique is more than simply offering feedback. Responding to other students' writing helps each writer develop his or her own writing proficiency. The value of a peer review session, then, is far greater than the sum of its parts, serving as a key stage in students' learning of criteria for effective writing in connection with the demands of specific tasks. Students should ultimately be able to apply this knowledge to their own writing as the scaffolds of peer response and support are removed, both in the later stages of writing this particular personal narrative and when writing other personal narratives. According to Joanna:

> The peer review process helped students notice what was missing in their own narratives as much as it pointed out the flaws in those of their peers. As they read through a peer's essay and commented on the depth of details, the organization, and the grammar, the students made references to their own compositions.

When they received their narratives back after a classmate's review, they were better able to begin revisions.

EPISODE 5.1. Have students, in their small groups, share their drafts of their narratives about a sense of place. Ask them to help one another identify sensory details that could be enhanced through vivid and evocative descriptions.

EPISODE 5.2. Ask students to create a new draft of their narrative in which these descriptions are included.

Stage 6. Paying Attention to Emotion

You also want your students to include how they feel about the place and/or experience they describe in their personal narrative. A number of musicians have written about places, real or imagined, that have great emotional importance to them, often in terms of the sense of home or refuge that it provides. When class time is precious, songs are a relatively brief means of exploring the ways in which authors tie themselves emotionally to places. The songs listed below delineate a range of places and the emotions associated with them. If you would like to focus more specifically on your own state or region, a number of songs are listed at http://inquiryunlimited .org/x1/etoc/usa_songsusa.html and http://kentonville.net/archival/ lyrics/state-songs-lyrics-cites-america.html.

The Drifters, "Under the Boardwalk" and "Sand in my Shoes" (combined into one song by The Persuasions)

Emmylou Harris, "The Sweet Rolling Hills of West Virginia"

Keb' Mo', "More than One Way Home"

Gladys Knight and the Pips, "Midnight Train to Georgia"

John D. Loudermilk, "Tobacco Road" (Lou Rawls' version is a favorite)

The Persuasions, "Don't It Make You Want to Go Home"

John Pizzarelli, "I Like Jersey Best"

Bertha Raffetto, "Home Means Nevada"

Dwight Yoakam, "Readin', Writin', and Route 23"

EPISODE 6.1.   Have each student choose a song (or two) about a place; identify (1) how the singer feels about the place and (2) how they knew or inferred that feeling; discuss the songs in small groups; and then report to the class. Be aware that while some songs are unambiguous about how the songwriter feels (often warm and sentimental), others include ironic or ambivalent feelings. As preparation, you could first lead a whole-class discussion on a song. Once students understand the process, give small groups the opportunity to apply the strategies before you ask students to apply them independently.

EPISODE 6.2.   Make sure students not only identify the emotions in the songs but also understand how the singers and songwriters produced these emotional effects. Perhaps the singer used a particular tone to convey an emotion in conjunction with particular images. Perhaps he or she expressed an emotion directly ("I felt so lonely I could cry") or less directly ("The greatest man I never knew lived right down the hall"). Identifying and analyzing these techniques prepares them to create an emotional tie to the setting of their story, thus expressing their feelings about the experience.

EPISODE 6.3.   Have students, in small groups, discuss how to revise their draft narratives to include their emotional relationship with the setting. You might provide a chart or transparency listing the strategies for making an emotional connection with a place that they developed in their song analyses.

EPISODE 6.4.   Have students produce final drafts of their personal narratives set in an emotionally important place and share them with their group. Joanna reports:

> The music activity was very helpful in showing my students how words can convey emotion. The students were able to identify the emotion in the songs about Georgia; this identification then prompted a discussion about how they could convey emotion in their narratives, which was one of the requirements. In their

small groups, they conferred about how and where to include keys to why this location and this event were important to them. They then produced a final revision.

Leigh's revision of her narrative about visiting the graveyard is provided in Figure 2–4.

Figure 2–4. Leigh's Revision

As I walked past the tall oak tree, luke-warm tears begin to fall. I know I shouldn't cry but images of you fill my mind. I continue walking until I find my spot. Once there I set and start thinking about happy thoughts. All the memories shared, laughs giggled and little simple smiles we gave to each other. I seems like just yesterday I was sitting on you're lap as you told me stories about a princess and her prince. I know right now you're smiling down upon me like when I was three so with that I begin to speak.

I say "Hello" and tell you that "I miss you" but all I hear is silence. Silence that fills my mind and voids my thoughts. Then before I fully lose myself I return back to my one sided conversation. Where I continue to tell you about school, my social life and how I hope you're proud of me, but still no answer.

I search for answers from within. The only response I seek is that I suppose no matter what I do you'd want your little sunshine to be happy and fulfill her dreams even if they're crazy or ridiculous. And that you'd want me to enjoy even the smallest things in life whether it be the tiny flower growing between the concrete or being around family and friends to enjoy it all.

After seeking my answers I look around to see no-one there just empty space. It seems to be such a lonely place even though its filled with so many soulful individuals. This feeling of loneliness makes me begin to stand, but before I go I sing to you "You are my Sunshine" so you never forget I'm always thinking of you. I place beautiful flowers upon your grave, look up to the sky and simply say I love you. I'll be back soon although I know you're always watching. I take those steps then drive away.

Stage 7. Generating Task-Specific Evaluative Criteria

So that students understand how their narratives will be evaluated, you now help them assess a set of personal narratives and determine their strengths and weaknesses. Although we position this activity here, it could be presented at other stages of the writing process. It could be the very first thing students do, to get them thinking immediately about the components and qualities of strong narratives. It could be placed between the introductory activities and their first drafts, or just before they produce their final drafts. If you feel having students evaluate narratives works better at an earlier point in the sequence, teach it there. If you teach the same lessons to several classes, try different sequences with different classes. You'll discover which sequence works best within the context of your teaching.

A second variable is the relative quality of the texts on which to base the criteria you and your students develop for producing and evaluating their personal narratives. In Chapter 1, "The Hit" (Figure 1–4) is generally regarded as the best of the three narratives the students analyze and use as a model for their own writing. Here three narratives representing a variety of problems and quality are provided, each having strengths and weaknesses, none being a singularly strong model. Students must separate the qualities they feel are important from significant flaws. The first (Figure 2–5) is a five-paragraph essay that includes introductory and concluding paragraphs. There are no grammatical problems, but it is a dull telling of potentially exciting events. The second (Figure 2–6) is perhaps the liveliest of the three but also includes the most errors in form. The third (Figure 2–7) includes a number of florid descriptions of the senses; students have to decide whether they are appropriately descriptive or overwritten. The third piece also contains little narrative, relying instead on a catalogue of sensory experiences present at the location.

A final variable is the lens through which students evaluate the narratives. In the approach taken in Chapter 1, the readership is assumed to be relatively homogeneous. Here each small group evaluates the narratives from the perspective of a different set of

Figure 2–5. Writing Sample 1

My Fun and Weird Fishing Trip
by Carson Truxx

I will tell you a story about a time I went fishing at my favorite lake. I will describe how I caught one crappie, one pickerel, and one seagull. Based on my story you will see that I had a fun but weird day while fishing at my favorite lake one day.

The first fish that I caught was a crappie. To catch the crappie I used a worm that I found in the ground and stuck on a hook. I then threw the hook with the squiggly worm on it into the water, where it drifted around about 10 inches below my red and white bobber. A bunch of crappies gathered around the worm and nibbled on it until one of them swallowed the hook. I then yanked on my fishing rod and set the hook and reeled it in. I put it in my creel to cook later.

I then changed from live bait to an artificial lure that is called a popper because it floats on the surface and when you yank on it it pushes a big bubble ahead of it, because it's got like an open mouth in the front that creates bubbles when you yank on it. It's supposed to look like an injured frog or mouse or something that a pickerel will want to eat. I cast my popper about 20 times before a pickerel hit it when it was about ten feet from me. I yanked the fishing rod to set the hook and reeled it in. I put it in my creel to cook later.

Finally, I decided to try to catch another pickerel with a popper. I cast the lure way out and started to make it pop. Suddenly a seagull swooped down and caught it in its feet and flew away with it. All of the line ran out of my reel making a zinging sound as the seagull flew away. Finally, all of the line was gone and I had to go home with just one crappie and one pickerel for dinner.

As you can see, I had a fun but weird day fishing at my favorite fishing lake. I caught two fish, which was fun, but caught a seagull that flew away with my artificial lure and all of my fishing line, which was weird. Next time I go, I'll bring an extra spool of fishing line just in case.

Figure 2–6. Writing Sample 2

Under the Tracks
by Mandy Torpedoes

In the naborhood where I live there are train tracks that run from downtown out to the aerport. The tracks are elevaded so that the cars can drive on the streets without having to stop all the time. The strangest things can take place under the tracks where its often dark and mysterious. One day on my way home from school a friend invited me over to his appartment to play video games, so I went a different roote than I normally do. To get to his house, we had to pass under a long underpass where all of the lites had burned out or broake and had never been replaced. Gang graphiti covered all of the cold concrete walls. I couldn't read what it said since it was in some mysteryous code, but it seemed to be a warning saying, "Danger! Stay Out!!" But my friend Walt said that he went under these trax evry day and had never been threatened. So we entered the dark opening and began to make our way threw. A bunch of pijjins were gathered around a carkass and as we grew closer they began to flap their wings like vultures around the kill. As we got closer I began to smell the dead carkass of a giant rat, stanking away in the dank underpass. The pijjins flapped and fluttered as we got closer, sending floating bits of trash into the air and like conffetti at a parade into a cave. I felt the taste of ancient garbage in my mouth as we crept past the pijjins and their rat, and the overpass began to shudder as a train rumbled overhead. Suddenly we herd a sound behind us and we saw the sillouettes of two large men carrying bats enter the underpass. We screamed and began to ran. We ran all the way to Walt's house and scrambled inside without looking back. We were chaking as we went up to his room and sat down at his game station, where we played Grand Theft Auto until dark. This time I took the trane home.

Figure 2–7. Writing Sample 3

My Story, Set in a Place
by Wendell Blowhard

There's a park near my house where I like to spend a lot of time. It's very important to me because I've had many experiences there. This is the story of one of those times.

There's a big tree in the park that is as big as the Empire State Building. Its branches reach out like hands inviting birds to sit on them. In the summer the wind blows through the leaves and they rattle like rattlesnakes moving in for the kill. And in the winter they stand out against the blue or grey sky like a silhouette. When it's snowy, you can hardly hear a thing.

I like to sit under this tree and think. The tree's bark has been carved with many initials and symbols, like the drawings on a cave wall that tell people many years later what life was like back then. The smells around the tree are numerous, including the stinky odor of nearby garbage cans, the fresh smell of newly cut grass, and the delicious odor of the food from picnic baskets when people have lunch nearby.

Sitting in the grass beneath the tree can be an itchy experience when there are bugs around, or when the grass is long and tickly. And the tree bark is rough like sandpaper on my back when I lean back against it.

I love this place, and I go there often. It's a special place to me because of these memories.

readers. Considering the responses of varied audiences helps students see that the qualities for any type of writing are not necessarily universal but are, rather, a function of the degree to which an author is "in tune" with the expectations and standards of specific communities of readers.

EPISODE 7.1.   Have small groups of students rank the three essays. Provide the following instructions:

> With the members of your writing group, pretend you are one of the following sets of readers. Each group must represent a different set of readers—no duplicates allowed. Adopting the stance and values of the group of readers you represent, rank the three narratives—"My Fun and Weird Fishing Trip," "Under the Tracks," and "My Story, Set in a Place"—from best to worst from the perspective of those readers.

> 1. Assessors for the state writing test

> 2. English teachers at your school

> 3. Adult judges in a narrative writing contest

> 4. Teenaged judges from a school literary magazine who are evaluating the narratives to decide which, if any, will be included in the next issue

> 5. Judges for a writing contest sponsored by the Chamber of Commerce of the community in which the narrative is set

> 6. Readers of a magazine such as *Merlyn's Pen* or NCTE's *Teen Ink* that features young adult writing

> 7. The author's best friend who has received the narrative as part of a holiday update

> 8. College admissions officers reading the narratives as part of a college application

> As part of your ranking, you will need to explain why people in your designated community of readers would rank them in the order you have determined. What qualities would they value most? What problems would be most and least important to them?

EPISODE 7.2.   When the groups have completed their rankings, lead a discussion based on their decisions. Have each group identify the readership it represents, explain the values these people would apply to their evaluation, and then share its findings. Give other groups an opportunity to respond to the group's ranking. Record their answers on the board, a projected transparency, or a document camera, and pose questions as needed to help each group explain and defend their rankings.

Given that the different perspectives of the communities of readers in the different groups might produce different but equally justifiable rankings, try to reconcile the differences and arrive at a single rubric you will use to evaluate the students' sense-of-place narratives (consult http://rubistar.4teachers.org/ for ideas). Below Joanna describes how she and her students constructed the rubric shown in Figure 2–8:

> The students guided the process. I handed out copies of all three examples, and the students discussed the pros and cons of the pieces. I could tell they were waiting for the "exemplar" they were conditioned to expect. When they did not receive it, they were surprised. However, their astute comments allowed us to create a rubric for grading their compositions. We began our rubric with the pro list—organization, depth of description, and style. We added the grammar requirement from the con list, thus including all the categories that Georgia judges students' writing on—content, organization, style, and grammar.

Joanna adapted the activity to coordinate with the state writing test her students would take. Many teachers shy away from process-oriented instruction because they are under so much pressure to teach to various tests—in Georgia and many other states, seemingly a new test for every day of the school year. Joanna's variation allowed her to present this sequence of activities while still remaining sensitive to her teaching obligations,

EPISODE 7.3. If you wish, lead a class discussion on how to improve one of the three narratives used for the ranking activity. Then have students, in small groups, revise one of remaining two narratives. If still more practice is warranted, individual students could revise the narratives they've written during this sequence, applying their understanding of the evaluative criteria to their own stories.

Figure 2–8. Personal Narrative Rubric

Requirements	1	2	3	4	5
Purpose of Narrative	The setting is missing OR there is no story (just description)	The story seems unrelated to the setting OR there is little description of setting	The setting relates to only a small part of the story	The story has a unique setting that is somewhat detailed or somewhat related	The writer has produced an entertaining story related to specific location
Use of Description	There is little or no use of imagery	Few examples of imagery are included, and they are unrelated to story	Imagery is present but does not add to the narrative	Imagery is included throughout the narrative but is awkward	Imagery is included throughout; it adds to the meaning of story
Organization	There is one long paragraph that lacks a flow to the narration; there is no ending	There is no ending, and some paragraphs lack organization	The author has written at least two paragraphs, but the breaks are not in the best locations; the story lacks a clear ending	The author has written several paragraphs, but could have written a more conclusive ending	The author has written several paragraphs, and has placed the breaks at logical points; the story includes a clear and satisfying ending
Grammar and Mechanics	Several errors distract from meaning	The story includes several errors, a few major ones (comma splice or sentence fragment)	There are minor errors throughout the story	There are some errors, but they don't distract from meaning	There are few or no errors
Style	The story consists almost entirely of simple sentences; diction and sentence stems are repetitive	Sentence structure is mostly simple sentences; diction is repetitive	Sentence structure is repetitive; diction is occasionally varied	Sentence structure and diction are varied, but there is some repetition of style	The author's sentence structure, diction, and sentence stems are varied

Total: _____ × 4 = _____ out of 100

Comments:

Stage 8. Language Lesson: Compound Sentences

Short, staccato sentences often help build suspense, while longer sentences can slow action down. Being aware of sentence length and structure can help students create an appropriate mood in their narratives and link their ideas together effectively. Like the sequence detailed in Stage 7, this instruction can be presented at a different point in the sequence. Because we choose to stress issues of form later rather than earlier in an instructional sequence, we position it here. Your own situation will tell you whether emphasizing compound sentences is the most appropriate language lesson for your students and whether this spot in the sequence is the most appropriate place for presenting it.

EPISODE 8.1. Introduce the exercise in Figure 2–9 and have your students complete it.

EPISODE 8.2. Have students provide feedback on one another's combinations *or* ask them to turn their work in for you to evaluate *or* lead a class discussion about appropriate combinations of the sentences in the exercise.

EPISODE 8.3. Give students an opportunity, either in small groups or individually, to look for places in their narrative drafts to incorporate compound sentences or to punctuate existing compound sentences properly.

Stage 9. Producing Final Drafts

EPISODE 9.1. Have students create their final drafts, either in class or on their own time, depending on your particular circumstances.

EPISODE 9.2. Have students use the class-generated rubric to evaluate their narrative, or provide one additional round of small-group feedback based on the rubric.

EPISODE 9.3. Conduct a final evaluation and attach a grade. Many teachers prefer to do this themselves; some allow the students to

Figure 2–9. Sentence Combining Exercise—Compound Sentences

Below are two examples of how you could combine sentences to form compound sentences using coordinating conjunctions or a semicolon:

The chicken crossed the road. She did not return.

Sentence: The chicken crossed the road, but she did not return.

Waylon Guitar trimmed his nostril hairs. He is now ready to go to the prom.

Sentence: Waylon Guitar trimmed his nostril hairs, and he is now ready to go to the prom.

Each item below contains two sentences. Combine them into one sentence, using a coordinating conjunction (*and, but, for, nor, or, so,* and *yet*) or a semicolon (*;*). Always place a comma before the conjunction (but not before a semicolon!).

1. Felton Earthquake hiked up the mountain. He got tired halfway up.

2. He decided to rest. He sat on a rock.

3. The rock began to wobble. The rock began to roll.

4. Felton was too tired to notice. He went for an unanticipated ride.

5. The rock moved slowly at first. It eventually picked up speed.

6. Felton began to notice a breeze. He began to wonder what the heck was going on.

Figure 2–9. Sentence Combining Exercise—Compound Sentences (*continued*)

7. The scenery flashed by. Felton realized that he was being taken for a ride.

8. Felton decided that he needed to eject from his vehicle. He might get hurt.

9. The rock was headed for a gigantic tree. Felton needed to act quickly.

10. Felton leaped from the rock just before it smashed into smithereens. He landed on a cactus that was perfectly placed for his arrival.

assign a grade. Choose whichever approach works best in your school and classroom, using the rubric that the class has agreed on as the basis for their grades.

Extensions

1. Introduce students to further readings on a sense of place using materials such as those gathered at http://www.coe .uga.edu/~smago/VirtualLibrary/Unit_Outlines.htm#Sense OfPlace. Students can either read about a state other than the one in which they live or explore their own state. They might consider what kind of culture exists in the state as a whole or in regions or places within the state, what it means to be from the state, what sorts of images one associates with various parts of the state, the kinds of emotions that the state or its subregions evoke in people, and related issues. Further writing could include analytic essays

that identify themes and images associated with the state, blogs that reflect the state and what it affords one's quality of life, taxonomic writing that classifies images of the state according to region or type, personal essays that provide perspectives on the state, multigenre projects that provide a collage of images that may or may not depict the state in a consistent way, and similar explorations.

2. Have students take one of the narratives written in their small group and produce a brief drama based on it. They could either perform the play live for the class or record it and play it on a screen.

3. Have students take a narrative written by someone else in the class and write a *prequel*: a story that takes place before the narrative begins. They will need to consider what might have taken place in order to set the stage for the events the author has recounted.

4. Have students take a narrative written by someone else in the class and write a *sequel*: what might have happened next. They will need to consider the characters, events, setting, and other elements of the prior story in order to produce what follows.

5. Have students take an image from a personal narrative written by a classmate and transform it into another artistic medium: drawing, painting, pantomime, sculpture, performance art, graphic novel, song, spoken word performance, and so on. What is gained and what is lost when a new medium is used to interpret the experience?

6. Have students rewrite their narrative from a different perspective, such as another character in the story, an object with a dispassionate view of the events, or a person who is not part of the action. Changing perspectives requires students to recognize that the perspective of the narrator determines much about what is revealed in a story and how a story is told.

7. Have students create a storyboard for a television show, film, or video game based on their narratives, either by themselves or in groups.

8. Have groups of students create a soundtrack for one of the stories, either selecting music from their collections or composing new music to accompany the events. Doing so requires them to understand the emotional shifts of the story and underscore them with music.

9. Have students submit their narratives for competition or publication. Both print (e.g., *Teen Ink*, *Merlyn's Pen*) and online outlets are available. The National Council of Teachers of English and many state affiliates sponsor youth writing competitions leading to publication.

Summary

This sequence of activities focuses on specific strategies for highlighting sensory detail and conveying emotional responses related to a place or an experience, knowledge that can be applied to additional narrative or descriptive writing later in the year. Materials are either available in the classroom or pulled from the Internet. Students are actively engaged during class, engaging with the materials, generating criteria to guide their writing, critiquing one another's work, and drafting and revising their narratives.

The instruction moves from readily accessible and easily knowable material—pictures about the state in which they live—and moves through increasingly difficult tasks such as describing sensory detail in mundane objects and ultimately including sensory and emotional detail. The students, through social interaction, consider their own experiences and the details that make reading their narratives a more vivid experience. Classmates provide feedback and suggestions and in doing so develop knowledge that will serve them in their own writing. Students generate evaluation criteria by inductively ranking sample essays from a variety of perspectives, a process that teaches them about the relational nature of reading and writing within specific communities of readers. These criteria are available to the students before they submit their work for a formal assessment, with the rubric both guiding their writing and helping them understand the basis for your ultimate formal assessment.

On the whole, the instruction is carefully scaffolded to promote students' proficiency in areas specific to writing personal narratives. Although some of these strategies can be applied to different tasks with different sorts of readers, students learn that these imaginative descriptions, while beneficial in writing personal narratives, may be inappropriate in other writing. A lab report outlining a scientific procedure, for example, might be marked down for the ambiguous use of metaphors and other figurative language or for attributing emotions to the frog that was dissected. This strategic knowledge of writing procedures will serve students well in writing that they do for future occasions, purposes, and readers.

3

Writing Personal Narratives as Part of Thematic Units of Instruction

Even though writing personal narratives is often regarded as appropriate for younger students, while older students are thought to need to concentrate on more detached analytic writing, we see no reason for any student to stop writing stories, given the large role storytelling plays in the lives of most people. Then, too, a large part of the literature curricula from preschool through graduate school comprises narratives.

As writing teachers, we believe it's important for students to experience a range of writing at every grade level. As the other books in this series reveal, there are abundant ways to include fictional narratives, comparison and contrast essays, argumentative writing, research reports, and essays that define concepts in just about any curriculum. Within a school year of roughly eight units of four to six weeks, students can produce each type of writing we describe in each year of their secondary school education, along with other kinds of writing as well: parody; the genres they read in their literature curriculum (e.g., tall tales, heroic journeys, allegories, science fiction, and many others); various kinds of poems; plays; blogs; multimedia productions; and much else.

The instructional units suggested in this chapter have been selected with developmental and curricular issues in mind. Younger students explore topics related to the sorts of personal experiences they are having at roughly that point in their lives and have the opportunity to write about their own experiences in relation to that theme. As students mature, new sorts of issues and experiences are incorporated into the curriculum. At the same time, the curriculum itself has certain predictable features. Although the curriculum in grades seven through ten may be designed differently from school to school, the eleventh-grade curriculum tends to specify American literature along with American history, and the twelfth-grade curriculum typically focuses on British literature or perhaps world literature or humanities. The units included here for these last two years of high school reflect this common curricular sequence.

Our goal is to suggest the many possibilities for including personal narrative writing at each grade level, not to provide a detailed instructional sequence. We encourage you to treat these suggestions as a blueprint from which to build your own curriculum. Most of the lists of materials that follow include far more texts than can be covered in four to six weeks. Select whatever is appropriate to your situation or substitute as you see fit.

Seventh Grade: Peer Group Pressure

Seventh graders are often worried about being included and accepted socially by their peers and faced with pressures to conform to their friends' ways of thinking and acting. A unit on peer pressure is appropriate to the age and maturity levels of most seventh graders and can help them understand the bewildering influences they face in relation to attitudes and behavior on the margins of what they find acceptable. As part of the unit, students could write personal narratives that explore the ways in which they are pressured by others to become more socially acceptable and take on identities that may or may not align with the beliefs present in their home, school, and faith community. The unit as a whole may help middle schoolers sort out the pressures being exerted on them and understand better how they align themselves among their peers.

Possible questions to explore in both literature and personal experiences include:

1. What are the values of the group applying pressure?

2. Why have the group members adopted these values?

3. Why do they try to impose them?

4. In what ways is the literary protagonist or individual student different from the group?

5. How does the literary protagonist or individual student respond to the pressure?

6. How does the literary protagonist or individual student change during the story or personal experience?

7. Why do people join peer groups? Are adults different from children and young people in this regard?

Unit Designs

Terri Avery (van Sickle) and Jennifer Hood, "Peer Relations, Peer Influence and Conformity," available at www.coe.uga .edu/~smago/VirtualLibrary/Avery_Hood.pdf

Julia Bateman, "Gangs, Cliques, and Peer Pressure," available at www.coe.uga.edu/~smago/VirtualLibrary/Bateman.pdf

Bethany Bishop, "Recognizing Reductionism: Identifying the Stereotypes Placed on Individuals and Groups by Society," available at www.coe.uga.edu/~smago/VirtualLibrary/ Bishop.pdf

Anna Harman, "Analyzing Adolescent Pressures and Choices Through Young Adult Literature," available at www.coe.uga .edu/~smago/VirtualLibrary/FSU/FSU2009_Harman_Analyzin gAdolescentPressures&ChoicesThroughYAL.pdf

Yahshae Mainer, "The Faces of Evil: A Look into Adolescent Violence," available at www.coe.uga.edu/~smago/ VirtualLibrary/FSU/FSU2010_Mainer_Violence.pdf

ReadWriteThink Online Lesson Plan

Kathleen Benson Quinn, "A High-Interest Novel Helps Struggling Readers Confront Bullying in Schools" available at www.readwrite think.org/lessons/lesson_view.asp?id=390

Writing by Teenagers

Merlyn's Pen search engine (www.merlynspen.org/read/library.php) for writing by teens about conformity, fitting in, outsiders, peer pressure, popularity, fitting in, and being different

Short Stories

Leonid Andreyev, "Nippie"

James Gould Cozzens, "The Animals' Fair"

S. T. Hwang, "The Donkey Cart"

John Langdon, "The Blue Serge Suit"

Jean Stafford, "Bad Characters"

Elizabeth Taylor, "Mice and Birds and Boy"

Nicolas C. Vaca, "The Purchase"

Jessamyn West, "Live Life Deeply"

Novels

S. E. Hinton, *Rumble Fish*
            The Outsiders

Toni Morrison, *The Bluest Eye*

P. J. Peterson, *Corky and the Brothers Cool*

Plays

Reginald Rose, *Dino*

William Shakespeare, *Romeo and Juliet*

Films

The Breakfast Club

Colors

Pretty in Pink

Sixteen Candles

West Side Story

The Warriors

Video Games

Grand Theft Auto franchise

The Warriors

Saints Row franchise

Eighth Grade: Loss of Innocence

Eighth graders are growing in their understanding of the complex worlds in which they are immersed. They increasingly come in contact with a wider range of people whose motives may or may not coincide with their youthful interests and who may betray the trust invested in them. Often at this age, adolescents are beginning to experience a loss of faith in others to whom they have dedicated their loyalty or generosity. Exploring the topic of loss of innocence may help eighth graders come to terms with experiences of their own by seeing them reflected in the actions and thoughts of characters they encounter in the unit's texts.

Questions to explore in both literature and personal experiences include:

1. What is innocence?

2. In what ways is the literary protagonist or individual student originally "innocent"?

3. What causes the "fall" from innocence?

4. How is the literary protagonist or individual student affected by the fall?

5. Is the literary protagonist or individual student better or worse off? Why?

6. What has the literary protagonist or individual student learned from this experience?

Writing by Teenagers

Merlyn's Pen search engine (www.merlynspen.org/read/library .php) for writing by teens about innocence

Myths

Pandora's Box

Phaethon

Deirdre and the Sons of Usna

The Bible

The Creation and the Fall (Genesis 1–3)

Poems

Countee Cullen, "Youth Sings a Song of Rosebuds"

Edna St. Vincent Millay, "Childhood Is the Kingdom Where Nobody Dies"

Theodore Roethke, "Dirty Dinky"

Christina Rossetti, "The Goblin Market"

William Stafford, "In the Old Days, Time"

Dylan Thomas, "Fern Hill"

Short Stories

Nathaniel Hawthorne, "Egotism, or the Bosom Serpent"

Irwin Shaw, "Peter Two"

John Updike, "You'll Never Know, Dear, How Much I Love You"

Robert Penn Warren, "Blackberry Winter"

Novels

James Baldwin, *Go Tell It on the Mountain*

Forrest Carter, *The Education of Little Tree*

Fred Gipson, *Old Yeller*

Kristin Hunter, *God Bless the Child*

John Knowles, *A Separate Peace*

Marjorie Rawlings, *The Yearling*

J. D. Salinger, *The Catcher in the Rye*

Sister Souljah, *No Disrespect*

Betty Smith, *A Tree Grows in Brooklyn*

Wole Soyinka, *Ake: The Years of Childhood*

John Steinbeck, *The Red Pony*

Songs

Barenaked Ladies, "Pinch Me"

Johnny Clegg, "The Promise"

Kathy Mattea, "The Innocent Years"

Video Games

The Legend of Zelda: Ocarina of Time

Ninth Grade: The Outcast

A unit on the outcast spirals back to issues explored in both the loss-of-innocence and peer-group-pressure units. Students focus on why people are rejected by others for being threateningly different.

Students might have experienced being outcasts themselves, witnessed others being rejected, or even participated in rejecting someone from a social group. This experience may be explored from a variety of angles to help students understand different forms of rejection and their effects on both the person cast out and those responsible for abandoning him or her. This unit is a particularly good opportunity for students to write personal narratives about events they then rewrite from the perspective of another person.

Questions to explore in both literature and personal experiences include:

1. In what ways is the outcast different from society or a particular social group?

2. Why does society or a social group reject this character?

3. How much control does the person rejected have over the source of difference? Do you believe that this person would change, if possible, in order to conform to the expectations of others?

4. To what extent does the character reject himself or herself after being cast out by others?

5. How does the character feel about the source of difference that leads to the rejection?

6. How does the character feel about the rejection and the people responsible?

7. How does the character try to resolve this rejection?

8. What does the group that casts someone out gain and lose by their rejection?

Unit Designs

Mark A. Richardson, unit on *Stargirl*, available at www.coe .uga.edu/~smago/VirtualLibrary/Richardson_2009.pdf

Writing by Teenagers

Merlyn's Pen search engine (www.merlynspen.org/read/library .php) for writing by teens about conformity, fitting in, outsiders, peer pressure, popularity, and being different

Poems

Langston Hughes, "Brass Spittoons"

Edwin Arlington Robinson, "Mr. Flood's Party"

Isaac Rosenberg, "The Jew"

Siegfried Sassoon, "Does It Matter?"

Dylan Thomas, "The Hunchback in the Park"

Short Stories

Truman Capote, "Jug of Silver"

Paul Gallico, "The Snow Goose"

Maxim Gorky, "Her Lover"

Bret Harte, "The Outcasts of Poker Flat"

Margaret Laurence, "The Half Husky"

Richard Matheson, "Born of Man and Woman"

Alice Munro, "Red Dress, Day of the Butterfly"

Dorothy Parker, "Clothe the Naked"

I. L. Peretz, "The Outcast"

Richard Rovere, "Wallace"

Isaac Bashevis Singer, "Gimpel the Fool"

Novels

Charles Dickens, *Great Expectations*
David Copperfield

Rachel Field, *Hepatica Hawns*

Ann Petry, *The Street*

Betty Smith, *A Tree Grows in Brooklyn*

John Steinbeck, *Of Mice and Men*

Autobiography

Richard Wright, *Black Boy*

Plays

Bertolt Brecht, *Galileo*

Reginald Rose, *Thunder on Sycamore Street*

Tennessee Williams, *The Glass Menagerie*

Films

Pretty in Pink

Valley Girl

Song

Ludacris and Mary J. Blige, "Runaway Love"

Video Game

Prince of Persia Trilogy (The Sands of Time, Warrior Within, The Two Thrones)

Tenth Grade: Discrimination

Discrimination appears to be a standard feature of human society. People are discriminated against for matters beyond their control, such as their race or their place of birth, and for factors of their own choosing, such as their religion or their political beliefs. By tenth grade, many students have had experience with discrimination. They may be subject to curfews imposed on all teens because of the behavior of a few. They might subscribe to unpopular beliefs. They may be a member of a racial or cultural minority group within their broader community. Or they might bear ill will toward people for the conditions that set them apart.

A unit on discrimination can help young people gain greater clarity about why discrimination seems to be such a pervasive aspect of human life. Writing personal narratives can help them explore their own experiences with discrimination while placing their personal actions in the context of those of their classmates and of characters they come across in literature and other sorts of texts. Although the goal of creating a more humane society is no doubt beyond the attainment of any classroom of teenagers, helping them come to terms with the forms of discrimination they have encountered may help them clarify the way they view the world and the role their own actions take in making society safe and secure for others.

Questions to explore in both literature and personal experiences might include:

1. Why is the character being discriminated against?

2. In what ways is the character different from the group that's discriminating?

3. Does the character want to be accepted? Why or why not?

4. What forms of discrimination is the character subject to?

5. How is the character affected by discrimination?

6. How is the conflict resolved?

7. What in the environment leads to discrimination?

8. What makes discrimination more likely in one environment than in another?

Unit Designs

Jeff Deroshia, "Social Stratification and Discrimination," available at www.coe.uga.edu/~smago/VirtualLibrary/Deroshia.pdf

Julie E. Duke, "Will the Real Mockingbird Please Stand Up?," available at www.coe.uga.edu/~smago/VirtualLibrary/Duke_2009.pdf

Jessica Trehy, "To Kill a Mockingbird," available at www.coe.uga.edu/~smago/VirtualLibrary/FSU/FSU2009_Trehy_ToKillaMockingbird.pdf

Online Lesson Plans

ReadWriteThink

Traci Gardner, "Comic Makeovers: Examining Race, Class, Ethnicity, and Gender in the Media," available at www.readwritethink.org/lessons/lesson_view.asp?id=207

Mary E. Shea, "Giving Voice to Child Laborers Through Monologues," available at www.readwritethink.org/lessons/lesson_view.asp?id=289

Michelle, Ota, "Promoting Diversity in the Classroom and School Library Through Social Action," available at www.readwritethink.org/lessons/lesson_view.asp?id=317

Karen Foster, "Seeing Integration from Different Viewpoints," available at www.readwritethink.org/lessons/lesson_view.asp?id=816

Loraine Woodard, "Using Picture Books to Explore Identity, Stereotyping, and Discrimination," available at www.readwritethink.org/lessons/lesson_view.asp?id=952

Yale-New Haven Teachers Institute

Sandra K. Friday, "Gordon Parks' Photography: Breaking Down Racial Barriers with Real Life Stories," available at www.yale.edu/ynhti/curriculum/units/2006/1/06.01.04.x.html

Jacqueline Porter-Clinton, "African American History: A Photographic Record," available at www.yale.edu/ynhti/curriculum/units/2006/1/06.01.08.x.html

Paul E. Turtola, "The Blues Impulse in Drama: Lessons on Racial Pain," available at www.yale.edu/ynhti/curriculum/units/1997/5/97.05.10.x.html

Units on racism and nativism in American political culture, available at www.yale.edu/ynhti/curriculum/units/1994/4/

Learn NC

Daryl Walker and Judy Peele, "Respecting Differences," available at www.learnnc.org/lp/pages/3992

Lynn Carter, "Differences Across the Curriculum: Part 1," available at www.learnnc.org/lp/pages/3459

Lynn Carter, "Differences Across the Curriculum: Part 2," available at www.learnnc.org/lp/pages/3719

Burnetta, Barton, "Jim Crow and Segregation," available at www.learnnc.org/lp/pages/4050

Writing by Teenagers

Merlyn's Pen search engine (www.merlynspen.org/read/library .php) for writing by teens about the elderly, handicaps, poverty, prejudice, racism, slavery, and stereotypes

Poems

Maya Angelou, "On the Pulse of Morning"

Juanita Bell, "Indian Children Speak"

Peter Blue Cloud, "The Old Man's Lazy"

Elizabeth Brewster, "Jamie"

Langston Hughes, "Mother to Son"

Len Margaret, "Night School"

Elizabeth Nowlan, "He Sits Down on the Floor of a School for the Retarded"

J. G. Saxe, "The Six Blind Men"

Wole Soyinka, "Telephone Conversation"

Short Stories

Peter Abrahams, "Tell Freedom"

Ray Bradbury, "All Summer in a Day"

José Antonio Burciaga, "Romantic Nightmare"

Maria Campbell, "Play with Me"

Alfred Hutchinson, "Road to Ghana"

Shirley Jackson, "After You, My Dear Alphonse"

Dorothy M. Johnson, "A Man Called Horse"

Alex Le Guma, "Where Are You Walking Around, Man?"

Albert Luthuli, "The Dignity of Man"

Amado Muro, "Cecilia Rosa"

Piri Thomas, "Puerto Rican Paradise"

Kurt Vonnegut, "Harrison Bergeron"

Alice Walker, "Everyday Use"

Novels

Sherman Alexie, *Reservation Blues*
Indian Killer

Alan Ekhart, *A Sorrow in Our Hearts*

Ernest Gaines, *A Lesson Before Dying*

Donald Goines, *White Man's Justice, Black Man's Grief*

Bette Greene, *The Drowning of Stephan Jones*

David Griterson, *Snow Falling on Cedars*

S. E. Hinton, *The Outsiders*

Nora Zeal Hurston, *Their Eyes Were Watching God*

Harper Lee, *To Kill a Mockingbird*

Adrian C. Louis, *Skins*

Kamala Markandaya, *Nectar in a Sieve*

Toni Morrison, Beloved, *The Bluest Eye*

Mourning Dove, *Cogewea the Half-Blood*

Leslie Marmon Silko, *Ceremony*

Alice Walker, *The Color Purple*

Margaret Walker, *Jubilee*

Elie Weisel, *Night*

Richard Wright, *Native Son*

Nonfiction

Essays

James Baldwin, "The Discovery of What It Means to Be an American"

Langston Hughes, "Fooling Our White Folks"

Martin Luther King, Jr., "Letter from a Birmingham Jail"

Enriqueta Longauex y Vasquez, "The Mexican American Woman"

Saunders Redding, "American Negro Literature"

Books

Angie Debo, *And Still the Waters Run*

Melissa Fay Greene, *Praying for Sheetrock*

Studs Terkel, *Division Street: America*

Jack Weatherford, *Native Roots, Indian Givers*

Autobiography

Maya Angelou, *I Know Why the Caged Bird Sings*

Anne Frank, *Diary of a Young Girl*

Richard Wright, *Black Boy*

Plays

Lorraine Hansberry, *A Raisin in the Sun*

William Shakespeare, *Othello*

George Bernard Shaw, *Pygmalion*

August Wilson, *Ma Rainey's Black Bottom*

Films

Clearcut

Crash

Dance Me Outside

Do the Right Thing

Guess Who's Coming to Dinner?

In the Heat of the Night

The Long Walk Home

Once Were Warriors

Shindler's List

Smoke Signals

Swing Kids

A Soldier's Story

X-Men

Documentary Films

Eyes on the Prize series

How We Got Over

Martin Luther King, Jr.: From Memphis to Montgomery

Songs

Harry Belafonte, "Kwela (Listen to the Man)"

Johnny Clegg, "One (Hu)man, One Vote," "Inevitable Consequence of Progress," "Asimbonanga"

Billie Holiday, "Strange Fruit"

Bob Marley, "War"

Dave Matthews, "Cry Freedom"

The Weavers (and many others), "Sixteen Tons"

Vanessa Williams, "Colors of the Wind"

Video Game

Final Fantasy 7

Eleventh Grade: Cultural Conflict

In American history and literature, the nation is often celebrated as a "melting pot" of cultural harmony. And yet the current strife over the status of immigrants from Central and South America is just the latest indication that the melding of cultures involves conflicts that are often difficult to resolve. In prior generations similar conflicts followed from new waves of people who came in contact with those who were already here, from the earliest European explorers/invaders/settlers/interlopers to the enslaved labor force made up of African slaves and Native Americans to each successive immigrant population whether here by choice or circumstances. Even people from groups that appear to be similar often clash over political ideology, religion, regional traditions, and other facets of cultural difference.

A course in American literature could fruitfully explore these issues, both in students' own lives and in the lives of historical and fictional characters. Writing personal narratives can be among the critical texts students produce and read to inform their growing understanding of the source and nature of conflicts that originate in cultural differences. As is often the case with issues that require a sense of perspective, if students take their narratives and rewrite them from the point of view of an antagonist in a clash of cultures, they can perhaps learn why the differences have resulted in conflict and learn to empathize with their opponents' point of view.

Questions to explore in both literature and personal experiences include:

1. In what ways are the cultures different?

2. Is one culture more powerful than the other? If so, in what way?

3. In the author's view (including a student author), is one culture superior to the other? If so, in what ways?

4. Do you agree with the author's judgment? If so, why; if not, why not?

5. What is the outcome of the clash? Is the outcome "fair"? Why or why not?

6. How do characters change as a result of their experience with another culture?

7. How are the cultures themselves different as a result of having come in contact with one another?

Although the junior year traditionally concentrates on U.S. history and literature, the lists below include texts from international writers as well, should you wish to stretch your curriculum or teach the unit at another grade level.

Unit Designs

Brian Patrick, "Alternate Narratives: The Revision of Cultural Representation in Achebe's Things Fall Apart," available at www.coe.uga.edu/~smago/VirtualLibrary/Patrick_2008.pdf

Kelly Galloway, "Am I a 'Weapon of Massive Consumption'? Learning to Fire the Canon," available at www.coe.uga .edu/~smago/VirtualLibrary/Galloway_2010.pdf

Katie Rybakova, "Traveling in the World's Footsteps," available at www.coe.uga.edu/~smago/VirtualLibrary/FSU/ FSU2010_KatieRybakova_TravelingintheWorldsFootsteps.pdf

ReadWriteThink Online Lesson Plan

Renee H. Shea, "Exploring Language and Identity: Amy Tan's 'Mother Tongue' and Beyond," available at www.readwrite think.org/lessons/lesson_view.asp?id=910

Writing by Teenagers

Merlyn's Pen search engine (www.merlynspen.org/read/library .php) for writing by teens about culture/traditions

Teen Ink (http://teenink.com/Travel/index.php) for writing by teens about cultural experiences

Poems

Chrystos, "Not Vanishing"

Thomas Hardy, "The Man He Killed"

Wilfred Owen, "Anthem for Doomed Youth," "Strange Meeting"

Lenrie Peters, "Parachute"

David Rubadiri, "Stanley Meets Mutesa"

Short Stories

Chinua Achebe, "A Man of the People"

Pearl Buck, "The Frill"

Christopher Isherwood, "The Berlin Stories"

Rudyard Kipling, "The Man Who Would Be King"

Abioseh Nicol, "The Devil at Yolahun Bridge"

Opal Lee Popkes, "Zuma Chowt's Cave"

Luci Tapahonso, "The Snakeman"

Emma Lee Warrior, "Compatriots"

Novels

Sherman Alexie, *Reservation Blues*
Indian Killer

Mongo Beti, *Mission to Kala*

Joseph Conrad, *Heart of Darkness*

Euclides da Cunha, *Rebellion in the Backlands*

Cyprian Ekwensi, *People of the City*

E. M. Forster, *A Passage to India*

Ailou Gaup, *In Search of the Drum*

Nadine Gordimer, *Livingstone's Companions*

Graham Greene, *The Human Factor*

Henry James, *The American*

D. H. Lawrence, *The Plumed Serpent*

Adrian C. Louis, *Skins*

Mourning Dove, *Cogewea the Half-Blood*

John Munonye, *The Only Son*

George Orwell, *Burmese Days*

Susan Power, *The Grass Dancer*

Polingaysi Qoyawayma, *No Turning Back*

Paul Scott, *The Jewel in the Crown*
　　　　　The Day of the Scorpion
　　　　　The Towers of Silence
　　　　　A Division of the Spoils

Leslie Marmon Silko, *Ceremony*

Amy Tan, *Joy Luck Club*

Ngugi wa Thiongo, *The River Between*

Nonfiction

Essays

Nien Cheng, "Life and Death in Shanghai"

George Orwell, "Shooting an Elephant"

Mark Twain, "Innocents Abroad: or, The New Pilgrim's Progress"

Autobiographies

Edwidge Danticat, *Brother, I'm Dying*

Archie Fire Lame Deer, *Gift of Power: The Life and Teachings of a Lakota Medicine Man*

John Rogers, *Red World and White*

Songs

Johnny Clegg, "Third World Child," "Orphans of the Empire," "Impi"

Yindi Yothu, "Treaty," "Djäpana," "Stop That" (and many others)

Spoken Word

Daniel Beatty, "Duality Duel"

Julian Curry, "Niggers Niggas & Niggaz"

Vanessa Hidary, "The Hebrew Mamita"

Films

The Class

A Great Wall

Dances with Wolves

Once Upon a Time in China

Once Upon a Time in China II

Once Upon a Time in China III

Up the Yangtze

Who Am I?

The Wooden Camera

Graphic Novel/Manga

Henry Kiyama (Yoshitaka), *The Four Immigrants Manga: A Japanese Experience in San Francisco, 1904–1924*

Video Games

Grand Theft Auto franchise

Twelfth Grade: The Quest for Power

This unit explores power as depicted by Shakespeare in a set of canonical plays often taught in twelfth-grade British literature classes. By the twelfth grade, students have already been exposed to power struggles, from elections for student government and social positions to informal conflicts within teams and social groups for leadership roles to their growing awareness of the social and political conflicts in broader society about whose values and perspectives prevail. Most students recognize their own position in the power continuum and have begun to develop opinions about why some people are able to impose their wills on others to prevail in differences over how a social group or society ought to proceed.

In this unit high school seniors consider the role of power in their own lives by writing personal narratives related to their social experiences as they read *Macbeth, King Lear,* and/or *Julius Caesar,* Shakespeare's canonical dramas about power struggles. These plays involve epic battles over social supremacy that distill the complexity of the human will for control and authority. Although students' own experiences may not involve the life-and-death conflicts illustrated by Shakespeare, they often share the fundamental emotions and ambitions depicted by his characters in these plays. In light of the dramatic focus of this unit, students might convert their prose personal narratives into a theatrical performance.

Questions to explore in both literature and personal experiences include:

1. Why do people seek power?

2. What do people gain and lose by questing after power?

3. How are conflicts over positions of power resolved?

4. What other avenues of resolution are available but not attempted, and what might have been the consequences of other approaches?

5. What effect do people have on others through their quest for power?

6. How do characters from history, literature, and the arts illuminate current issues pertaining to power struggles?

Plays

William Shakespeare, *Macbeth, King Lear, Julius Caesar*

4

What Makes This a Structured Process Approach?

As we hope we have demonstrated in the pages of this book, we believe that kids learn best when actively engaged in activities that interest them. This premise is the foundation of a structured process approach. Now that you have seen what teaching this way looks like, we'll lay out the basic principles that guided our planning and that might guide yours, too, going forward:

- The teacher usually identifies the task, such as writing a personal narrative, although students may participate in deciding what they want to learn how to write. Even with the task identified, students often begin learning the processes involved by participating in simple activities such as describing a shoe in enough detail that it can be identified in a pile of footwear.

- Learning begins with *activity* rather than with the product of that learning. For example, in the shoe activity in Chapter 1, students use hands-on (or, in this case, feet-on) materials and critique one another's descriptions.

- The teacher designs and sequences activities that allow students to move through increasingly challenging problems of the same type. For example, in Chapter 1, after writing about their own shoes, students write about less familiar objects such as seashells, marbles, or apples.

- Students' learning is highly social, involving continual talk with one another as they learn procedures and strategies for particular kinds of writing. In Chapter 1, small groups of students discuss the details of their shell, decide what to include in their description and how to present it, and attempt to identify another group's shell.

- The teacher designs the activities that take students through the particular writing process that produces the final product. However, in class, *the students are the ones talking and doing.* The teacher's role is primarily to help students apply the strategies, not to exercise a heavy hand in leading discussions and guiding the writing. The scaffolding provided by Joanna Anglin in Chapter 2 illustrates how a teacher manages these interactions effectively.

A structured process approach therefore places the teacher in the role of designer and orchestrator of student activity through which the *students themselves* make many of the decisions about how to write and how to assess the quality of their writing. Figure 4–1 is a more comprehensive list of principles that guide this approach. We and other teachers influenced by George Hillocks have outlined this approach in a number of publications, including Hillocks (1975, 2006), Hillocks, McCabe, and McCampbell (1971), Johannessen, Kahn, and Walter (1982, 2009), Kahn, Walter, and Johannessen (1984), Lee (1993), McCann, Johannessen, Kahn, Smagorinsky, and Smith (2005), Smagorinsky (2008), and Smagorinsky, McCann, and Kern (1987). Several of these titles are available for free download at www.coe.uga.edu/~smago/Books/Free_Downloadable_Books.htm.

Designing Structured Process Instruction

A structured process approach to teaching writing involves two key ideas: *environmental teaching* and *inquiry instruction* (Hillocks 1995).

Figure 4–1. Principles of a Structured Process Approach

1. Instruction allows students to develop procedures for how to compose in relation to particular kinds of tasks. The processes that students use to write comparison/contrast essays, for example, are different from those used to write personal narratives.

2. Because different tasks require different procedures, writing instruction cannot rely solely on general strategies. Rather than simply learning "prewriting" as an all-purpose strategy, students learn how to prewrite in connection with a specific genre—writing a personal narrative, for example, in which case small groups of students might explore the narrative possibilities suggested by particular experiences.

3. With writing instruction focused on specific tasks, students work toward clear and specific goals with a particular community of readers in mind. A personal experience written for a group of their friends might be quite different from one written for the general public. Each readership expects different rhetorical features and responds differently to interpersonal issues.

4. Even with clear and specific goals, thinking and writing are open-ended. Story content, structure, diction, and other elements vary from writer to writer, depending on one's knowledge, the nature of the experience being recounted, and one's audience.

5. Composing is a highly social act, rather than the work of an individual. Students discuss their compositions with peers at every stage of development. In a structured process approach, people learn to write by *talking* as well as by writing.

(continues)

Figure 4–1. Principles of a Structured Process Approach (*continued*)

6. The teacher and students share an understanding of the criteria used to assess the writing. Students often help develop these evaluative criteria by discussing what they value in the writing they read. When the writing is tied to large-scale assessment, such as writing narratives for a district or state gateway exam, the criteria may already be in place.

7. The teacher *scaffolds* students' learning of procedures by designing activities and providing materials that the students may manipulate. Initial instruction is simple and manageable. For example, when learning how to write personal narratives, students might first explore familiar material through informal writing. Instruction then progresses through more challenging aspects of the writing, such as refining word choices. Attention to form comes later in the instruction when students have developed content to write about, rather than earlier, as is often the case with instruction in how to write the five-paragraph theme and other forms.

8. When possible, the teacher provides additional readerships for students' writing, such as having the students post their writing in the classroom or on a classroom wiki or submit their writing to a contest, the school newspaper, the school literary magazine, and so on.

Environmental Teaching

One important assumption that underlies environmental teaching is the belief that *each task we ask students to do involves unique ways of thinking*. By way of example, think of what is involved in three types of writing tasks: defining effective leadership, comparing and contrasting two leaders, and writing a personal narrative about providing leadership. Each relies on different ways of thinking and communicating one's thinking in writing, and each involves different rhetorical features. An environmental approach, then, stresses learning particular sets of *procedures* for engaging in specific sorts of *tasks* so as to produce a *form* that meets the expectations of readers.

To help students learn to accomplish a new task, a teacher needs to involve students directly in developing strategies for undertaking that task. In other words, the teacher introduces activities that will help students learn *how* to do this new kind of thinking and writing.

A task in this sense involves both *doing* something and *thinking about how it's done* so that it can be done again with different materials. A task, then, may comprise writing a personal narrative, or comparing and contrasting similar yet different things, or arguing in favor of a solution, or defining a complex concept such as progress or success. Our goal for students is that when they complete this task, they are able to repeat the process more independently the next time by applying their procedural and strategic knowledge to new material.

Inquiry Instruction

Inquiry is the particular structure through which students work, often in collaboration with one another.

Again, the teacher plays a strong role designing activities that provide the basis for students' inquiries into the problems they investigate. For personal narratives, the problem may be *how* to identify suitable experiences to write about and then how to transform one's memories of those experiences into compelling writing.

The students play with materials related to the questions they hope to settle through their writing. *Play* in this sense refers to experimenting with ideas, and while it may involve a great deal of fun, may also be quite serious. For example, students explore possible topics for their narratives in the safety of a small group, under the teacher's radar. They play with language to come up with the best way to capture the essence of an experience, sorting through any number of word choices, many of which will be discarded. They bounce alternate beginnings and endings, for different readerships, off their peers. They might create analogies ("the shape of this seashell is like a tornado"), try out ideas they later reject, respond to and extend one another's ideas, and otherwise experiment collaboratively before drafting their narrative.

Students' work is open-ended in that the activities may have many plausible solutions or outcomes. One student might write about coming of age because of a wrenching experience. Others may find such a topic too painful and choose something more entertaining and less consequential. Small-group discussions allow students to play with these ideas and try out solutions that may or may not ultimately figure into the final decision.

Applying Structured Process Instruction

This book illustrates how you might put these principles into practice when teaching students to write personal narratives. By deliberately working through the various stages required to complete an immediate product, your students have an opportunity to write narratives that matter to them and that gradually improve in quality. The process of producing these narratives contributes to their understanding of their experiences. With their explicit knowledge of thinking and writing procedures, they will be able to apply them to other situations involving personal narrative writing when they work independently. Students address a particular problem, work with specific problem-solving strategies, and rehearse their writing in discussions with other students before they put their ideas on paper.

What Can You Expect When Teaching Writing with This Approach?

Preparing students to write well-developed, thoughtful narratives is time-consuming for both you and your students. The detailed, systematic process outlined in this book sequences students' progress through procedures for both thinking about and writing a personal narrative. The activities cannot attend to *all* the considerations in completing a task this complicated and interactive, and often other imperatives from the curriculum constrain the time available to teach any ability thoroughly and effectively. Realistically, before students are able to apply specific skills and strategies to new situations, they will need several experiences and appropriate feedback from you, from other students, and if possible from other readers. However, with continual reinforcement, the procedures that students generate should enable them to write strong personal narratives on future occasions when they choose or are called upon to create them.

Where Do You Go from Here?

This book and the others in this series provide specific plans you can adapt to your own teaching. They also introduce you to a process you can use to design original instruction based on your classroom and your students' needs. The guide below will help you design writing instruction using a structured process approach:

1. *Identify the task that will form the basis for your instruction.* Assuming that any general process such as "prewriting" differs depending on the demands of particular writing tasks, identify the task that will form the basis of the instruction. This task might be specified by a formal writing requirement and assessment provided by a mandate from the school, district, or state (e.g., argumentation); it might be writing that you believe is essential in your students' education (e.g., research reports); it might be writing that students identify as something they want to learn how to do (e.g., college application essays); or it might come from some other source or inspiration.

2. *Conduct an inventory of students' present writing qualities and needs.* With the task identified, you will probably want to see what students' writing of this sort looks like prior to instruction. Doing so allows you to focus on students' needs and avoid teaching strategies they already know. You could take this inventory by providing a prompt like, *Write about a personal experience in a place of significance to you. Tell your story so that it is clear why this place is important to your experiences. Make sure that your readers will be able to see, hear, smell, touch, and taste the environment and experience your emotions about the place along with you. Be as*

specific as you can in describing the event and its consequences or impact. Then assess their abilities in relation to your *task analysis*, which we describe next.

3. *Conduct a task analysis.* Either by consulting existing sources or by going through the processes involved in carrying out the writing task yourself, identify what students need to know in order to write effectively according to the demands of readers. The task analysis should treat both *form* (e.g., the use of quotation marks to indicate a speaker's words) and *procedure* (e.g., how to describe smells in order to create an evocative setting). The task analysis will also help you identify the evaluative criteria that you ultimately use to assess student work.

4. *Conduct an activity analysis.* Determine the types of activities that will engage students with materials that are likely to foster their understanding of the processes involved in the task. Identify familiar and accessible materials they can manipulate (e.g., items already present in the classroom, like the shoes they are wearing, or that you provide, like seashells) for the early stages of their learning, and introduce more complex concepts (e.g., approaching the experience from varied perspectives) for subsequent activities.

5. *Design and sequence students' learning experiences so that they provide a scaffold.* Design increasingly challenging tasks of the same sort using increasingly complex materials. Sequence these activities so that students are always reiterating the process but doing so in the face of greater challenges. The activities should present continual opportunities for students to talk with one another as they learn the processes involved in carrying out the task.

6. *Consider opportunities to teach language usage in the context of learning procedures for task-related writing.* Specific kinds of writing often benefit from particular language strategies. For example, students need to learn ways to identify

the source or speaker of direct quotations and other information. Targeting language instruction to specific instances of its use helps overcome the problem inherent in discrete grammar instruction, which is that it fails to improve students' understanding of how to speak and write clearly.

7. *Relying on the task analysis, develop rubrics through which students clearly understand the expectations for their writing.* These rubrics may be developed in consultation with students, adopted from established criteria such as those provided for state writing tests or advanced placement exams, adopted from model rubrics available on the Internet, created by examining a set of student work that represents a range of performance, and so on.

8. *Provide many opportunities during the learning process for feedback and revision.* Students should be given many occasions to get feedback on drafts of their writing. This feedback can come by way of peer response groups, your written response to their writing, writing conferences with you, or other means.

A Structured Process Approach and Professional Learning Communities

Currently many school faculties constitute a professional learning community made up of collaborative teams. Structured process instruction is particularly effective in this context. Teachers together develop instruction and analyze student work. Teams use the student writing produced during the instructional sequence as a basis for discussing what worked, what students are struggling with, and what should be done differently or what needs to be added. They collaboratively design rubrics for scoring student work so that expectations for students are consistent. Collecting data on student performance from pretest to final product allows the group to evaluate student growth, reflect on the strengths and weaknesses of the instruction, and plan future classroom activities.

Our own teaching has shown us that this approach can greatly improve students' writing over the course of instruction. We look forward to hearing how you have adopted this approach to your own teaching and helped your students learn how to use written expression to meet their responsibilities as students, writers, friends, communicators, and citizens.

Questions for Reflection

1. How would you respond to colleagues who believe that writing stories is for kids, and that in middle and secondary school, students should be learning analytical skills primarily and writing exposition, argumentation, and literary criticism essays rather than personal narratives?

2. How does the assessment context affect the degree to which you can teach the processes involved in different sorts of writing tasks? How can you teach using a structured process approach, which takes more class time than just assigning and grading papers, in an already overcrowded curriculum?

3. Are there any sorts of narratives that you should discourage students from writing, or is students' personal need to express themselves paramount, regardless of the propriety of their topics, events, and language?

4. How will you manage occasions when students' stories seem to be cries for help, such as stories of abuse, illegal activities, and the like?

5. If your class includes English language learners whose English fluency is low but whose native language fluency is high, to what degree will you enable them to write their narratives in both their first and second languages?

6. To what degree should the literature from anthologies provide models for students' own narrative writing?

7. This book includes sentence combining activities designed to help students with particular kinds of sentence structures involved in narrative writing. What other kinds of language instruction could you include in your teaching of personal narrative writing?

8. How could technology be incorporated in helping students learn to write personal narratives?

9. How could blogs, wikis, or other interactive technology be used in helping students as they learn to write personal narratives?

10. What activities would you develop to help students reflect on the thinking and writing processes they used in writing personal narratives?

11. When you are evaluating students' personal narratives, what kinds of comments do you think are most helpful to students? What kinds of comments would be least helpful? What specific comments and/or suggestions would you make for the student who wrote the various stories in Chapters 1 and 2 that students evaluate to generate the criteria by which they will be evaluated?

12. Some educators are highly critical of rubrics because, they believe, rubrics are inflexible and lead to rote grading. How can you use rubrics so that they do not handcuff writers or evaluators of personal narratives?

References

Bruner, J. 1986. *Actual Minds, Possible Worlds*. Cambridge, MA: Harvard University Press.

Duke, N. K. 2000. "3.6 Minutes per Day: The Scarcity of Informational Texts in First Grade." *Reading Research Quarterly* 35: 202–24.

Hillocks, G. 1975. *Observing and Writing*. Urbana, IL: National Council of Teachers of English. Retrieved December 6, 2008 from www.coe.uga.edu/~smago/Books/Observing_and_Writing.pdf.

———. 1986. *Research on Written Composition: New Directions for Teaching*. Urbana, IL: National Conference on Research in English and Educational Resources Information Center.

———. 1995. *Teaching Writing as Reflective Practice*. New York: Teachers College Press.

———. 2002. *The Testing Trap: How State Writing Assessments Control Learning*. New York: Teachers College Press.

———. 2006. *Narrative Writing: Learning a New Model for Teaching*. Portsmouth, NH: Heinemann.

Hillocks, G., E. Kahn, and L. Johannessen. 1983. "Teaching Defining Strategies as a Mode of Inquiry." *Research in the Teaching of English* 17: 275–84.

Hillocks, G., B. McCabe, and J. McCampbell. 1971. *The Dynamics of English Instruction, Grades 7–12*. New York: Random House. Retrieved August 4, 2006 from www.coe.uga.edu/~smago/Books/Dynamics/Dynamics_home.htm.

Johannessen, L. R., E. Kahn, and C. C. Walter. 1982. *Designing and Sequencing Prewriting Activities*. Urbana, IL: National Council of Teachers of English. Retrieved July 2, 2008 from www.coe.uga.edu/~smago/Books/Designing_and_Sequencing.pdf.

———. 2009. *Writing About Literature.* 2d ed. Urbana, IL: National Council of Teachers of English.

Kahn, E., C., C. Walter, and L. R. Johannessen. 1984. *Writing About Literature.* Urbana, IL: National Council of Teachers of English.

Lee, C. D. 1993. *Signifying as a Scaffold for Literary Interpretation: The Pedagogical Implications of an African American Discourse Genre.* Urbana, IL National Council of Teachers of English.

Loewen, J. W., and E. H. Sebesta, eds. 2010. *The Confederate and Neo-Confederate Reader: The Great Truth About the Lost Cause.* Jackson, MS: University Press of Mississippi.

McCann, T. M., L. R. Johannessen, E. Kahn, P. Smagorinsky, and M. W. Smith, eds. 2005. *Reflective Teaching, Reflective Learning: How to Develop Critically Engaged Readers, Writers, and Speakers.* Portsmouth, NH: Heinemann.

Smagorinsky, P. 1991. "The Writer's Knowledge and the Writing Process: A Protocol Analysis." *Research in the Teaching of English* 25: 339–64.

———. 2008. *Teaching English by Design: How to Create and Carry Out Instructional Units.* Portsmouth, NH: Heinemann.

Smagorinsky, P., T. McCann, and S. Kern. 1987. *Explorations: Introductory Activities for Literature and Composition, Grades 7–12.* Urbana, IL: National Council of Teachers of English. Retrieved December 8, 2008 from www.coe.uga.edu/~smago/Books/Explorations.pdf.

Smith, M. W. 1989. "Teaching the Interpretation of Irony in Poetry." *Research in the Teaching of English* 23: 254–72.

Weaver, C. 1996. *Teaching Grammar in Context.* Portsmouth, NH: Heinemann.

Teaching Students to Write

The Dynamics of Writing Instruction series

- ▶ **Argument**
- ▶ **Essays That Define**
- ▶ **Comparison/Contrast Essays**
- ▶ **Personal Narratives**
- ▶ **Research Reports**
- ▶ **Fictional Narratives**

Designed to provide teachers with resources that ensure students gain the writing skills needed for success in college and careers

"These books will support teachers in their understanding of designing process-based instruction and give them both useful lesson plans and a process for designing instruction on their own that follows the design principles."

—Peter Smagorinsky, Larry Johannessen,
Elizabeth Kahn, and Thomas McCann

Argument / Grades 6–12 / 978-0-325-03400-3 / 2011 / 96pp est. / $14.50
Essays That Define / Grades 6–12 / 978-0-325-03401-0 / 2011 / 96pp est. / $14.50
Comparison/Contrast Essays / Grades 6–12 / 978-0-325-03398-3 / Spring 2012 / 96pp est. / $14.50
Personal Narratives / Grades 6–12 / 978-0-325-03397-6 / Spring 2012 / 96pp est. / $14.50
Research Reports / Grades 6–12 / 978-0-325-03402-7 / Spring 2012 / 96pp est. / $14.50
Fictional Narratives / Grades 6–12 / 978-0-325-03399-0 / Spring 2012 / 96pp est. / $14.50

CALL **800.225.5800** WEB **Heinemann.com** FAX **877.231.6980**   DEDICATED TO TEACHERS